Criminal Justice
Recent Scholarship

Edited by
Nicholas P. Lovrich

A Series from LFB Scholarly

Lethal Violence and Religion

Institutional and Denominational Effects on Homicide and Suicides in U.S. Counties

Bryan K. Robinson

LFB Scholarly Publishing LLC
El Paso 2015

Library of Congress Cataloging-in-Publication Data

Library of Congress Cataloging-in-Publication Data

Robinson, Bryan K., 1976-
Lethal violence and religion : institutional and denominational effects on homicide and suicides in U.S. counties / Bryan K. Robinson.
pages cm. -- (Criminal justice: recent scholarship)
Includes bibliographical references and index.
ISBN 978-1-59332-769-9 (hardcover : alk. paper)
1. Violence--Religious aspects. 2. Crime--Religious aspects. 3. Homicide--United States. 4. Suicide--United States. 5. Crime--United States--Sociological aspects. I. Title.
BL65.V55R63 2015
364.152088'2--dc23
2014039077

ISBN 978-1-59332-769-9

Manufactured in the United States of America.

Dedicated to my grandparents

Table of Contents

Acknowledgments

While a list of all those whose support and inspiration made this research monograph possible might well exceed the length of the document, there are a handful of individuals who deserve special mention. First, and most important, I would like to thank my spouse Amelia for her patience and understanding throughout the protracted process of research conducted for this book. Next, I would like to thank Steven Messner, Ryan King and Glenna Spitze, for their collective and individual guidance and inspiration. I would also like to thank Betty Ann Hughes for her tenacious proofreading and Erica Hunter, Warren Sheldon and Larry Rafflovich for their moral support and advice. Finally, I thank my family – Sandy Sudduth, Larry Robinson, Kathy Robinson, Don Sudduth, Doris Light and James Robinson – for their emotional and financial support.

CHAPTER 1:

Lethal Violence in the United States

The Centers for Disease Control and Prevention (CDC) (2012) estimates that 50,000 lives are lost each year to violence in the United States. In 2010, the CDC (2014) recorded 12.4 suicides per 100,000 U.S. residents, and the Federal Bureau of Investigation (FBI) (2011) recorded 4.8 murders per 100,000 U.S. residents. Considered within a global context, these statistics are alarming; the homicide rate in the United States is 6.9 times greater than the average homicide rate of all other high-income countries (Richardson and Hemenway 2011). Moreover, while suicide ranks 13th and homicide ranks 22nd as leading causes of mortality in the world (Mercy, Krug, Dahlberg, and Zwi 2003), they rank 10th and 15th, respectively, as leading causes of mortality in the United States (Minino, Murphy, Xu, and Kochanek 2011). In fact, in every year since 1965 both homicide and suicide have appeared among the top 15 leading causes of death in the United States (Dahlberg and Mercy 2009).

High rates of family disruption, economic inequality, firearm availability, alcohol consumption, and secularization have each been identified as likely factors in causing elevated community suicide rates (Stack 2000a; Stack 2000b) and homicide rates (see McCall, Land, and Parker 2010; Miller, Azrael, and Hemenway 2002; Norstrom 2011). Despite these similarities, community homicide and suicide rates often diverge on some key characteristics, including urbanization (suicide is more prevalent in rural counties (Singh 2002) while homicide is more prevalent in urban counties (Kowalski and Duffield 1990)) and geographic region (suicide is highest in the western portion of the country and lowest in the northeast (Shrira and Christenfeld 2010) while homicide is strongly correlated with the south (Lee, Bankston, Hayes, and Thomas 2007)). To explain some of these regional differences, scholars have theorized that religion may play a central role (e.g., Ellision, Burr, and McCall 2003; Stark and Bainbridge 1996). Better understanding the causes of regional differences could lead to significant reductions in lethal violence; Papadopoulos, Skalkidou, Sergentanis, Kyllekidis, Ekselius, and Petridou (2009) estimate that if the suicide and homicide rates in each region of the United States could be reduced to the rates found in the Northeast, roughly 12,000 lives could be saved annually.

It is also important to consider the economic and social toll generated by unusually high lethal violence rates in the United States, both directly through increased medical costs, legal costs, and the loss of productive members of society (Beeghley 2003), and indirectly through increased public fear, anxiety, and depression (Zimring and Hawkins 1997). For example, estimates place the annual loss in worker productivity and medical cost to lethal violence at around $52.4 billion (Corso, Mercy, Simon, Finkelstein, and Miller 2007). Specifically, each murder is estimated to cost society an average of $1.2 million in worker productivity losses and criminal justice system costs (McCollister, French, and Fang 2010). Suicide can also disrupt family cohesion and increase the risk of suicide among surviving family members (Cerel, Jordan, and Duberstein 2008), while homicides have been linked to increased risk of post-traumatic stress disorder (PTSD) among the victim's family and friends (Hertz, Prothrow-Stith, and Chery 2009).

Given these alarming statistics, public health officials have begun to examine both suicide and homicide more deeply as epidemiological issues (Hammond, Whitaker, Lutzker, Mercy, and Chin 2006; Rosenberg, O'Carroll, and Powell 1992). A common tactic adopted in public health research involves studying homicide and suicide together as a single phenomenon (i.e., as lethal violence). Although this approach is deeply rooted in the sociological and criminological literatures, it is not a widely accepted strategy in either field of study. One central objective of this research monograph is to assess any explanatory advantages of using an integrated model of lethal violence versus the more common criminological and sociological practices of examining homicide and suicide as separate and distinct phenomena.

Over the last century, academics have treated suicide and homicide as two distinct forms of violent death, and this differentiation has persisted throughout modern sociological and criminological literature. As a consequence markedly different theoretical explanations and divergent policy recommendations have developed for these two forms of lethal violence. One notable exception can be found in Unnithan, Huff-Corzine, Corzine and Whitt's (1994) treatise on the merits of investigating lethal violence in a unified manner.

The Unnithan et al. (1994) integrated model revolves around two key synergistic concepts – namely, "forces of production" and "forces of direction." These researchers define the former as any variable that accounts for an increased volume in the overall lethal violence rate, and the latter as any variable that increases the likelihood of lethal violence manifesting as either suicide or homicide. One advantage of the integrated model is that it provides a framework for recognizing and appreciating similarities and differences among correlates of homicide and suicide. For example, both forms of lethal violence have been correlated with measures of economic inequality, family structure, and religious affiliation. Although Unnithan et al. investigated economic inequality's impact on both suicide and homicide in their book, and other scholars have examined the role of family structure on lethal violence (e.g., He, Cao, Wells, and Maguire 2003), no research has yet explored religion's role as a force of production. Similarly, the integrated model provides an analytical framework with which to understand discrepancies between the homicide and suicide literatures. Unnithan et al. demonstrated this by examining regional differences in the United States as a possible force of direction that could account for high homicide and low suicide rates in the South, but low homicide and high suicide rates in the North. While recent research in sociology and public health epidemiology has explored such regional differences, both in the United States and abroad, little research has been conducted to identify and investigate other forces of direction, including religion, which Unnithan et al. identify as a potential factor at play in regional differences.

Another limitation of contemporary research, especially within the public health literature, is that despite a strong focus on statistical analysis and policy, there appears to be limited application of the full theoretical potential of Unnithan et al.'s integrated model. In particular, few if any public health scholars have used Unnithan et al.'s research as anything more than a blanket justification for analyzing suicide and homicide as an aggregated concept. Consequently, these researchers have failed to take advantage of the key theoretical implication of the integrated model -- namely, the importance of analyzing the synergistic nature of forces of production and forces of direction. Studies focusing on forces of production or forces of direction alone are shortsighted because, as Unnithan et al. point out, there are a myriad of reasons why an increase or decrease in the lethal violence rate may create the illusion that suicide and homicide rates are positively correlated, inversely correlated, or uncorrelated.

A few contemporary scholars in sociology and criminology have utilized Unnithan et al.'s approach more fully to examine issues ranging from gender differences in lethal violence (Batton 2004; Vollum and Titterington 2001) to the influence of family structure and cohort size on lethal violence (O'Brien and Stockard 2006). More recently, Nielsen and Martinez (2009) investigated the impact of immigration rates on lethal violence rates among African Americans and Hispanics in Miami while Lanier (2010) employed the integrated model to better understand lethal violence among Native Americans. Each of these studies further demonstrated the utility of the integrated model by showing both the versatility of the approach and demonstrating the model's ability to repeatedly bring new insights beyond those of previous work that has focused only on suicide or homicide individually.

Past tests of the integrated model have examined the influence of economic, geographic, and family demographic measures on lethal violence; however, religion, one of the key variables in both homicide and suicide research, has been thus far overlooked. There are several important reasons for employing the integrated model to examine religion's influence on lethal violence, including: the prominence of religion in both fields; the opportunity to reconcile disagreements as to whether homicide and suicide vary inversely or directly in various religious environments; and, the potential to merge two of the major theoretical traditions under one model.

Historically, religion has held a prominent role in sociological investigations into suicide (e.g., Durkheim [1897] 1979; Stack 2000b; Wray, Colen, and Pescosolido 2011). Recently, criminologists have begun to call for more attention to connections between religion and crime (e.g., Akers 2010; Cullen 2010; Desmond, Kikuchi, and Morgan

2010; DiIulio 2009; Johnson and Jang 2010). While each field of study has developed radically different policy approaches to its respective piece of the lethal violence puzzle, each relies on rather similar variables and quite similar theoretical explanations that lend themselves to analysis through an integrated model.

Moreover, recent theoretical trends in both homicide and suicide research have focused on social networks as key elements in explaining religion's influence on rates of each. For example, Pescosolido and Georgianna (1989) proposed a network-based interpretation of Durkheim's theory that attributes low suicide rates among Catholics and evangelical Protestants to the well-integrated and protective nature of the social networks that they develop. On the other hand, Beyerlein and Hipp (2005) attributed higher homicide rates among evangelical Protestants to the tight-knit integration of their social networks. Despite these divergent findings, no one has offered any clear theoretical justification for why these religiously-based networks might have opposing effects on homicide and suicide. One possible solution to this anomaly can be tested with the integrated model. In particular, if homicide and suicide are opposing channels within the same stream, then highly integrated networks like those found in evangelical Protestant communities might encourage higher rates of externalized aggression rates by fostering an "us versus them" mentality; they may also simultaneously discourage suicidal behavior by encouraging stronger ties among members within each network.

The integrated model also allows for a synthesis between institutional-based and denominational-based explanations of religion's influence on antisocial behavior. Macro-sociological research on religion's impact on homicide or suicide has thus far focused either on the overall religiosity of the community, or on the denominational composition of the community. Scholars focusing on institutional influences exerted by community religiosity have generally expected religion to reduce both homicide and suicide, while scholars focusing on denominational differences have predicted divergent trajectories for religion's influence on homicide and suicide. By shifting to the integrated model, it is possible to re-frame these two theoretical approaches: one as an explanation of the forces that produce lethal violence in a community, and the other as a predictor of whether that lethal violence will more likely manifest as homicides or suicides. Thus, religious institutional strength will act as a force of production, while denominational composition will act as a force of direction within the integrated model framework.

Beyond the theoretical contribution of the integrated model remains an important question: what are the policy implications of researchers' examinations of lethal violence? Since contemporary scholars have chosen to study homicide and suicide independently, it is not surprising that current United States' policies tend toward punitive measures to reduce homicide rates and therapeutic measures to reduce suicide rates (O'Brien and Stockard 2006). However, as increasing support is found for a holistic understanding of lethal violence, policy approaches to the different types of lethal violence may also become less bifurcated. In particular, the macro-sociological approach of the integrated model is ideally suited for identifying early warning signs that would allow policy makers to work toward preventive measures, in contrast to the current reactionary, punitive and treatment-based policy approaches (Stockard 2003). If homicide and suicide are interlinked as the integrated model suggests, then disaggregated approaches to lethal violence may lead to ineffective policies that merely reduce one form of lethal violence while simultaneously increasing the other. Using the broader lens of the integrated model to identify forces of production and forces of direction, however, allows for theory-informed policy suggestions that can successfully reduce both homicide and suicide rates.

Drawing from the Association of Statisticians of American Religious Bodies' (2002) research on religious congregations and the CDC's vital statistic records on lethal violence between 1999 and 2002, this project will examine religion's influence on county-level rates of lethal violence using Ordinary-Least Squares (OLS) regression analysis. In particular, three predictive models will be estimated: one for the influence of community religiosity on lethal violence; another for the influence of denominational composition on lethal violence; and a third and final model for the influence of the interaction between community religiosity and denominational composition on lethal violence.

The next chapter will review the theoretical literature surrounding the integrated model, explaining both its historical roots and its contemporary applications. Chapter 3 will examine the differences between the institutional effects literature and the denominational effects literature and their approaches to linking religion and lethal violence rates. That chapter will present three models: one testing the institutional effects of religion; one testing the denominational effects of religion; and a final model derived from merging the institutional effects and denominational effects literature with the integrated model. Next, chapter 4 will lay out specific hypotheses and explicate the current study's methodological strategies. Chapters 5 and 6 will discuss the findings of the institutional effects model, the denominational effects model and the interaction model, respectively. Finally, chapter 7 will draw final conclusions and propose fruitful avenues for future research.

CHAPTER 2:

The Integrated Model of Lethal Violence

The purpose of this chapter is to explore the historical foundations of the integrated model of lethal violence, present its contemporary formulation, and provide a detailed account of its recent applications. The first section of this chapter will summarize the historical development of the integrated model. The second section will focus on the theoretical underpinnings of the integrated model; reflecting primarily on the work of Unnithan, Huff-Corzine, Corzine and Whitt, it will detail the theory itself along with both the methodological and policymaking advantages provided by this approach. The third and final section of this chapter will review recent empirical applications of the integrated model and discuss the gaps and problems left by this literature.

THEORETICAL FOUNDATIONS: PRECURSORS OF THE INTEGRATED MODEL

In the mid-1990s, Unnithan, Huff-Corzine, Corzine and Whitt (1994) revived a pre-Durkheimian strategy of studying homicide and suicide as two facets of the same underlying phenomenon (i.e., lethal violence). In their extensive historical review of the literature, they point to the early19th century moral statisticians Enrico Morselli and Enrico Ferri as the first theorists to lobby for an integrated approach. Moreover, they identify Emile Durkheim as the detractor who first popularized the disaggregated approach that is still practiced in modern research. In many respects, Unnithan et al.'s work can best be described as assembly rather than discovery. Where they contribute to the integrated model is by bringing together three separate concepts -- Morselli and Ferri's integrated approach, Durkheim's stream analogy, and Henry and Short's frustration/aggression hypothesis -- into a single unified theory.

According to Unnithan et al. (1994), the genesis of the modern integrated model lies in the early works of moral statisticians Morselli and Ferri, both of whom independently ". . . characterized the relationship between homicide and suicide as involving parallelism in their underlying causes but contrast in their modes of expression" (p. 16). These two early scholars were responding to a range of descriptive studies that demonstrated an inverse relationship between suicide and homicide. For example, research by Guerry ([1833] 2002) had identified high rates of suicide and low rates of homicide in northern regions, but high rates of homicide and low rates of suicide in southern regions of Europe. Similarly, Morselli noted the following: "The regions and States which are pre-eminent in crimes of blood are indeed those where suicide is scarce. . . " ([1881] 1903:149). While Morselli and Ferri were not the first to embrace this view, they were pivotal in evangelizing it during a time period when criminology first began to take hold as a social science. Unnithan et al. pointed to Morselli's keynote speech and Ferri's presentation at the First International Congress of Criminal Anthropology held in Rome in 1885 as examples of their commitment to a unified study of homicide and suicide. Although their ideas did not go unchallenged at the time, it was not until the publication of Durkheim's seminal work *Le Suicide* that mainstream criminology and sociology would begin to reject their approach.

Durkheim's ([1897] 1979) response to Morselli and Ferri is relevant for two reasons. First, as mentioned above, it ultimately set a research agenda in the social sciences that abandoned the integrated model in favor of a disaggregated approach to lethal violence. Second, the analogy that Durkheim provides to describe Morselli and Ferri's theoretical position became a centerpiece of the modern integrated theory's explanation. What becomes known as 'the stream analogy' or 'stream theory' is first presented in *Le Suicide* as follows:

> But this antagonism, once granted, may be explained in either of two ways. Either homicide and suicide form two opposite currents, so opposed that one can gain only through the other's

> loss, or they are two different channels of a single stream, fed by a single source, which consequently cannot move in one direction without receding to an equal extent in the other. (Durkheim [1897] 1979:340)

Durkheim goes on to reject the integrated approach by arguing that suicide and homicide do not consistently act in opposite directions in every case:

> By way of summary, then, suicide sometimes coexists with homicide, sometimes they are mutually exclusive; sometimes they react under the same conditions in the same way, sometimes in opposite ways, and the antagonistic cases are the most numerous. How explain [sic] these apparently contradictory facts?
>
> The only way to reconcile them is by admitting that there are different sorts of suicide, some of which have a certain kinship to homicide, while it is repugnant to others. For the identical phenomenon cannot possibly behave so differently under the same circumstances. The suicide which varies in the same proportion with murder and that which varies inversely with it cannot be of like nature. (P. 355)

What is perplexing about Durkheim's application of the stream analogy is his narrow focus on only the variance between homicide and suicide. He does not consider the interaction between the source of the violence in the stream and which channel it takes. This oversight was not addressed until a century later, at which point Unnithan and colleagues developed the modern version of the integrated model. Furthermore, Durkheim's stake in developing a theory of suicide may have influenced his critique, thus leading him to dismiss the integrated model in favor of one that could more easily meld with his typology of suicide:

> We thus reach the following conclusion. If suicide and homicide often vary inversely to one another, it is not because they are two different aspects of the same phenomenon; but because in some respects they form two opposed social currents. In these respects they are as mutually exclusive as

> day and night, just as the diseases of extreme drought preclude those of extreme humidity. If this general opposition still does not completely prevent harmony, it is because certain types of suicide, instead of depending on causes opposed to those which occasion homicide, are on the contrary expressions of the same social condition and develop in the midst of the same moral environment. Besides, it may be anticipated that homicides which coexist with anomic suicide and those which are reconcilable with altruistic suicide cannot be of the same nature; that homicide, therefore, like suicide is not a single, indivisible criminological entity, but must include a variety of species very different from one another. But this is not the place to dwell on this important proposition of criminology. (Durkheim [1897] 1979:358)

It is possible, however, to reconcile Durkheim's theory of suicide with the modern integrated model, as done recently by O'Brien and Stockard (2006) by recasting integration and regulation as forces of production. Henry and Short (1954) first laid the groundwork for this synthesis by developing an explanation for the choice between suicide and homicide based on levels of integration.

As its third major historical component, Unnithan et al.'s integrated model incorporated Henry and Short's theory on lethal violence, developed primarily from Freudian psychology and based on the two psychological states of frustration and aggression:

> In suicide, the target of the aggression is the self. In homicide, the target of the aggression is another person. We concluded that the choice of target for the aggression was in part a function of the strength of external restraint over behavior. When behavior is required to conform rigidly to the demands and expectations of other persons, the probability of suicide as a response to frustration is low and the probability of homicide as a response to frustration is high. When behavior is freed from the requirement for conformity to the demands and expectations of others, the probability of suicide is high and the probability of homicide is low . . . . (Henry and Short 1954:101-102)

> . . . both suicide and homicide react in the same way to one objective source of frustration—loss of status consequent to the flow of economic forces. And in our discussion of the sociological and psychological bases of legitimacy of other-oriented aggression we have specified certain of the factors which determine whether the aggression consequent to the frustration is directed inwardly against the self or outwardly against others. (P. 119)

For Henry and Short, the two key elements in explaining the variance between homicide and suicide are frustration and social integration. More specifically, they argued that both suicide and homicide are types of aggression caused by similar forces of frustration (e.g., economic inequality), but that individuals' decisions to cope with that frustration through suicide or homicide is linked to the amount of restraint placed on them by society:

> When behavior is subjected to strong external restraints by virtue either of subordinate status or intense involvement in social relationships with other person, the restraining objects can be blamed for frustration, thereby legitimizing outward expression of the resultant aggression. When behavior is freed from external restraint, the self must bear the responsibility for frustration. (Henry and Short 1954:103)

Consequently, individuals experiencing high levels of social integration (e.g., middle class, married and whites) would be more likely to commit suicide in the face of increased frustration, while those experiencing low levels of social integration (e.g., lower class, divorced and African Americans) would be more likely to commit homicide. Developing this frustration/aggression hypothesis further, Gold (1958) theorizes that cultures that accept and utilize physical punishments in response to deviant behavior would be more likely to produce members who externalize blame while those that focused on psychological punishments would generate more internal blame. For example, Gold points out that the lower class may be more prone to homicide given higher rates of corporal punishment in low income families, while the middle class may favor suicide given its preference for psychological strategies of child rearing. These two versions of the integrated model, however, rely heavily on micro-psychological processes and continue the assumption made by Durkheim that suicide and homicide must vary inversely for the integrated model to be of use.

SYNOPSIS OF THE INTEGRATED MODEL

The key component of Unnithan et al.'s integrated model is the idea that the variables influencing lethal violence (homicide and suicide) can be segregated into two separate causal groups. First, 'forces of production' comprise variables that influence the overall amount of lethal violence that occurs in a given geographic area. Second, 'forces of direction' consist of variables that determine the likelihood that lethal violence will manifest either externally as homicide or internally as suicide. By shifting the focus from a separate analysis of either suicide or homicide, which limits researchers to investigating forces of production only, to a more holistic analysis of lethal violence, the integrated model allows for a deeper understanding of each variable's role in both producing and directing both suicide and homicide rates in communities. This approach has a further benefit of informing public policy actors by helping separate variables that influence the overall violence rate from variables that only reduce one form of lethal violence, possibly at the expense of increasing the risk of another.

Elaborating on the 'stream analogy' concept Unnithan et al. provided the following summary of the integrated model:

> The total volume of "water" in the stream is represented in the integrated model by the lethal violence rate, or LVR, defined as the sum of the suicide rate and the homicide rate. Symbolically,
>
> $$LVR = S + H,$$
>
> Where S = the number of suicides per one-hundred thousand people, and H = the number of homicides per one-hundred thousand people. The choice between suicide and homicide is represented by the suicide-homicide ratio, or SHR, obtained by dividing the suicide rate by the sum of the suicide rate and the homicide rate (that is, the LVR). Thus,

> SHR = S/(S + H).
>
> The task for research based on the integrated model is to identify the two sets of variables that act, respectively, as forces of production and forces of direction. (1994:96)

Unnithan et al. interpreted the stream analogy differently from Durkheim and many other scholars by recognizing the influence of the volume of lethal violence in the stream on the two divergent paths of homicide and suicide. While Durkheim's critique of the stream model focused exclusively on the alternating currents, Unnithan et al. pointed out that the suicide-homicide ratio is very dependent on the lethal violence rate. Consequently, Durkheim's core argument that the steam theory is inadequate hinges on his belief that lethal violence ". . . cannot move in one direction without receding to an equal extent in the other" ([1897] 1979:340). This interpretation, however, is flawed since it assumes that the violence rate remains constant. Under Unnithan et al.'s interpretation of stream theory, homicide and suicide only vary inversely when the suicide-homicide ratio plays a stronger role than do the forces of production responsible for generating lethal violence:

> There are nonetheless several implications for the study of suicide and homicide rates that follow from viewing lethal violence in terms of the integrated model and the stream analogy that underlies it. First, if variables in the set contributing to the production of lethal violence drop to such low levels that the stream dries up, there will be no suicide and no homicide, regardless of the magnitude of those variables that affect attributions of blame and are thereby responsible for the division of water into the two channels. Second, even if the stream has an ample supply of water due to the operation of forces of production, there will be no suicide if all the water is diverted into one channel, and no homicide if it is all directed into the other. While neither of these hypothetical situations is even remotely approached in large, real-world populations, they illustrate the point that both suicide and homicide rates depend upon both forces of production and those of direction. (1994:98)

Thus, the stream analogy depends on two heavily interdependent parts – namely, the volume of the stream itself, and the forces that influence the diversion of the stream into one channel or the other. If researchers only examine the relationship between homicide and suicide without taking into account the volume of lethal violence, then they risk misinterpreting the relationship between these two variables:

> An additional implication, which is not only nonobvious but counterintuitive as well, is that if the integrated model is correct, it is possible for either suicide rates or homicide rates, but not both, to vary inversely with frustration. It is also possible for suicide rates to vary directly with external attributions of blame or for homicide rates to vary directly with internal explanatory styles. These relationships, of course, are precisely the opposite of what we would expect on the basis of most theories of suicide and homicide . . . . (Unnithan, Huff-Corzine, Corzine, and Whitt 1994:100)

Durkheim is not the only scholar to mistakenly oversimplify the stream analogy. In their interpretation of the Gestalt shift brought about by the integrated model, Lester and Yang described it as simply querying, "How violent are societies, and in which direction do they direct their aggression . . . ?" (1998:32). But this explanation is deceptively oversimplified. While it is true that one of the key uses of the integrated model is its potential for identifying forces of production and forces of direction, neither of these processes can be successfully tested for independently. Because of the synergistic nature of the integrated model, it is essential to remember that just as examining suicide or homicide independently may lead to misclassification of variables as force of production or direction, so too could independent analysis of the lethal violence rate or suicide-homicide ratio lead to misinterpretations of the interconnected nature of suicide and homicide rates. While Lester and Yang failed to cite Unnithan et al., they did include an analysis of the influence of divorce rates and out-of-wedlock birth rates on both the production and direction of lethal violence in 19 countries over the period 1950 to 1985. They reported the following: "Nations with high divorce rates and low marriage rates tend to experience higher rates of both lethal violence and inwardly-directed violence" (p. 37). Moreover, they found "tentative evidence that nations with higher birth rates also had higher rates of inwardly-directed violence" (p. 37), but found no clear evidence of a connection between birth rates and lethal violence. Lester and Yang also examined the association between homicide and suicide rates across nations, finding that "countries with higher rates of homicide tend to have higher rates of suicide" (p. 42); they argued that the finding refutes the notion that these two phenomena are opposing outcomes for the same causal variables.

Unfortunately, this is a clear example of misinterpreting the integrated model by focusing only on the suicide-homicide ratio. The assumption made by Lester and Yang (also made by Durkheim) is that for the stream analogy to be correct, suicide and homicide can only operate in an alternating fashion; that is if one increases then the other must decrease. However, this assumption fails to take into account the synergistic nature of the integrated model. By leaving out the lethal violence rate, it assumes that any given increase in suicide or homicide must be accompanied by a decrease in the other form of violence. Taken as a whole, however, the integrated model appropriately allows for simultaneous increases and decreases in both homicide and suicide by recognizing that the homicide and suicide rates are not just dependent on the factors that direct violence inwardly or outwardly, but also on the factors that increase or decrease the overall volume of lethal violence. As Unnithan et al. explained:

> If forces of production remain constant while those of direction change, the relationship between homicide and suicide will be negative because the increased flow of water into one channel is diverted from the other. On the other hand, if forces of direction are held constant and, consequently, the relative sizes of the two channels remain unchanged, both channels will increase or decrease proportionately with any change in the total volume of water in the stream; and the relationship between suicide and homicide will be positive. (1994:99)

In further modernizing the integrated model, Unnithan et al. identified basic theoretical explanations for the forces of production and forces of direction hypothesized to be at play. They linked forces of production, as did Henry and Short, with the concept of frustration.

Unlike Henry and Short, however, Unnithan et al. focused exclusively on macro-sociological processes, steering clear of individual levels of frustration in favor of widespread sources of frustration. For Unnithan et al., the suicide-homicide ratio is a ". . . product of situational and cultural factors that contribute to the development of explanatory styles which include causal explanations of bad events (frustrations) . . ." (p. 97). Here, they moved away from Henry and Short's focus on measures of integration in favor of a more culturally aware notion of attribution processes. They go on to assert that ". . . forces of production are typically sought in socially patterned sources of frustration, stress, or negative life events such as structurally based economic inequality and anomie . . ." (p. 96), and that forces of direction include ". . . structural conditions and cultural patterns that affect the attribution of responsibility for frustration" (p. 96-97).

Accounting for both forces of production and forces of direction allows researchers to better understand the relationships between variables influencing lethal violence. For example, research conducted on homicide rates or suicide rates individually could easily mistake a force of direction as a force of production. This misidentification could then lead to ineffective policy decisions that focus on reducing homicide or suicide in ways that only shift the direction of violence between these two types of lethal violence. Similarly, research conducted on disaggregated lethal violence rates could underestimate or overestimate the influence of a force of production if forces of direction are not properly accounted for:

> . . . the integrated model leads to a number of nonobvious conclusions that suggest that studies of either suicide or homicide rates in isolation from one another may overlook important factors that can affect their results. For example, the integrated model predicts that the attribution of blame for bad events has a greater effect on both suicide and homicide rates in settings characterized by high levels of frustration than it does in less frustrating environments. Similarly, frustration should have a greater effect on suicide rates than on homicide rates under conditions in which persons are culturally predisposed to take responsibility for their own bad outcomes. Conversely, frustration should be more closely correlated to homicide than to suicide rates under structural and cultural

> conditions encouraging external attributions of blame. (Unnithan, Huff-Corzine, Corzine, and Whitt 1994:100)

It is easy to imagine a scenario in which policy decisions based on homicide or suicide rates alone would prove problematic. For example, if variable A has a strong negative relationship with the suicide-homicide ratio but no influence on the lethal violence rate, that variable could appear in homicide-centric models as positively correlated with the homicide rate and in suicide-centric models as negatively correlated with suicide rates. Consequently, policy decisions based on the homicide-centric model might step up efforts to reduce homicide at the expense of increasing suicide, while suicide-centric models might encourage policies that reduce suicide but encourage homicide. Meanwhile, only the integrated model would recognize that variable A is unrelated to the root problem of lethal violence and realize that policy decisions based on this variable would only serve to shift the direction of violence back and forth between suicide and homicide.

FINDINGS IN THE ORIGINAL STATEMENT OF THE INTEGRATED MODEL

In their book *The Currents of Lethal Violence* Unnithan et al. (1994) conducted two empirical tests of their proposed integrated model. The first test examined economic inequality as a structural condition, while the second focused on regional cultural differences in lethal violence. Both empirical tests were presented in an attempt to highlight the complex interaction between forces of production and forces of direction.

In order to demonstrate the advantages of the integrated model, Unnithan et al. weighed in on the debate over the influence of inequality and economic development on lethal violence. First, they pointed to the lack of agreement on whether inequality's relationship with lethal violence is linear or nonlinear. They also noted that previous studies have identified divergent effects of economic development on suicide and homicide, creating an unresolved issue in the literature.

Approaching these issues from the lens of the integrated model, Unnithan et al. hypothesized that inequality would increase the lethal violence rate by bolstering levels of frustration for a majority of the population while simultaneously decreasing the suicide-homicide ratio as the general population attributed these frustrations to the external sources of inequality. They further hypothesized that increased economic development would lead to increases in the suicide-homicide ratio: "As the industrial process brings the forces of nature under human control, personal blame for perceived failure is more likely to be placed on the self" (1994:120). Essentially, for Unnithan et al., unjust economic conditions lead to increased levels of frustration, which in turn produce higher rates of lethal violence. The inequity of the system also encourages the externalization of blame, which leads to declines in the suicide-homicide ratio as violence is more likely to be expressed toward others. On the other hand, economic development brings about higher levels of perceived control over everyday life, which in turn increases the likelihood that individuals will accept responsibility for their success and failures leads to increases in the suicide-homicide ratio as aggression manifests internally as suicide.

Examining cross-national lethal violence rates (in both integrated and disaggregated forms) for 88 countries, Unnithan et al. conducted ordinary least squares (OLS) regressions relying on Gross National Product (GNP) for their measure of economic development and the income share of the highest quintile as their measure of inequality. They found support for the integrated model by demonstrating that while inequality is significantly correlated to cross-national homicide and suicide rates and economic development is significantly related to suicide, there is no significant relationship between either of these variables and the lethal violence rate. Furthermore, they found a strong and significant correlation between both inequality and economic development and the suicide-homicide ratio. Specifically, they found a negative linear relationship between inequality and the suicide-homicide ratio and a positive linear relationship between economic development and the suicide-homicide ratio. Moreover, they noted that the R^2 for the two independent variables' effect on the suicide-homicide ratio was equal to .429, while the values for the suicide and homicide models were .411 and .249, respectively.

> If we posit a reality in which suicide and homicide are causally separate phenomena, our analysis has established that (1) suicide rates increase with development independently of inequality, but once inequality is controlled, the inverse relationship between homicide and economic development

> disappears; (2) suicide rates decrease and homicide rates increase with inequality, independent of economic development; (3) the relationship between development and suicide is curvilinear with a generally increasing curve, independent of inequality; and (4) the relationship between suicide and inequality is curvilinear with a generally decreasing curve, independent of development.
>
> Shifting gears to accommodate the alternative reality of the stream analogy, our findings indicate that (1) the total amount of lethal violence is generally unrelated to either economic development or inequality; (2) as inequality increases, lethal violence is more likely to be directed against external targets than toward oneself; and (3) the greater the economic development, the greater the probability that lethal violence will be turned against the self as suicide. (1994:141)

While Unnithan et al. quickly pointed out that neither of the above set of findings is technically wrong, since both contain the same information and simply represent two different ways of viewing the data, they did however recognize the value of simplifying explanations for homicide and suicide into a single model in the spirit of Ockham's razor. Further, while the integrated model does not provide any new information about the lethal violence rate that is not available in disaggregated models of the suicide rate and homicide rate, it does contain useful information about the suicide-homicide ratio that cannot be obtained (as explained above) by disaggregated models.

Unnithan et al. further explored the relative merits of their integrated model by investigating regional influences on lethal violence in 48 U.S. states; in particular, they examined the well-documented relationship between the southern region of the United States and elevated homicide rates. They proposed that by expanding the focus from simply studying homicide to looking at lethal violence via the integrated model, it may be possible to gain a deeper understanding into the cultural and structural forces involved in southern violence. They note that prior regional research focused on homicide rates had failed to generate consistent support for either structural explanations (e.g., poverty) or cultural explanations (e.g., southernness). As with their previous research on economic inequality, Unnithan et al. hypothesized that ". . . high rates of severe poverty are positively related to the LVR for both blacks and whites" (p. 149) given the increased levels of frustration brought about by inequitable systems. As for regional differences that cannot be attributed to economic differences, Unnithan et al. draw from prior researchers' use of the southern subculture of violence to hypothesize about regional influence on the suicide-homicide ratio. Specifically, they hypothesized that Southern culture would be inversely related to the suicide-homicide ratio. They base this speculative expectation on both historical factors (civil war and reconstruction) and religious factors (in particular, Protestant fundamentalism) that should plausibly foster high levels of external blaming.

Examining African Americans and whites separately, Unnithan et al. tested the impact of a structural poverty index and the percent of the population born in the census-designated South region on the lethal violence rate and the suicide-homicide ratio for each state. Among whites, Unnithan et al. found the strongest predictor of the lethal violence rate to be the structural poverty index, which was also positively correlated with the suicide-homicide ratio, a finding which they concluded highlights poverty's role in increasing both lethal violence and the pressure toward internalized aggression. They also found no evidence of a connection between percent born in the South and increased lethal violence rates. However, they did find a significant negative correlation between percent born in the South and the suicide-homicide ratio, which they contend demonstrates that Southern culture may play a pivotal role in directing lethal violence externally toward homicides but has no effect on the net lethal violence rate for whites. Among African Americans, they found a significant positive relationship between the structural poverty index and lethal violence rate, but no relationship between percent born in the South and the lethal violence rates. Their findings for African Americans also indicate no significant relationship between the structural poverty index and the suicide-homicide ratio, and a significant negative correlation between southerness and the suicide-homicide ratio.

Both sets of findings support the integrated model by demonstrating the valuable insights provided by the inclusion of the suicide-homicide ratio. Prior research focusing exclusively on homicide or suicide would not have fully explicated the scope of poverty's role in increasing lethal violence, or classified the role of cultural and historical conditions in the South in directing that violence externally in the form of high homicide rates and low suicide rates. Consequently, Unnithan and colleagues end their book with a call for a revival of the integrated approach to lethal violence research in the hopes of even further clarifying the interlocking nature of homicide and suicide rates

APPLICATIONS, TESTS AND REVISIONS OF THE INTEGRATED MODEL

Since Unnithan et al.'s reintroduction of the integrated model, only a handful of studies have utilized their approach to lethal violence. These studies can easily be divided into applications of the integrated model, tests of the integrated model, and attempts to theoretically fine-tune the model.

Empirical Applications of the Integrated Model

Although Unnithan et al.'s reformulation of the integrated model would appear to offer great promise, it has not been widely adopted by the sociological/criminological community. In fact, prior to 2000, only two studies adopted this approach to studying suicide and homicide. The first study was a short piece by Lester and Leenaars (1998) that analyzed suicide rates and homicide rates separately, despite their discussion of the utility of Unnithan et al.'s integrated approach. The second study was a primarily interpretive piece carried out by Singh and Unnithan (1999) that attempted to illustrate the value of the integrated model in explaining the structural frustration and cultural attribution styles that led to two cases of spouse burning in the United States.

In the first full implementation of the integrated model, Vollum and Titterington (2001) examined gender differences in lethal violence by identifying divergent attribution styles characterizing women and men. Referring to the attribution literature, Vollum and Titterington pointed to a multitude of prior studies that link increased likelihood of external attribution of blame to males and internal attribution of blame to females. They hypothesized that gender would play a critical role in the suicide-homicide ratio, with women being more likely to manifest violence as suicides and men as homicides. Utilizing the integrated model, Vollum and Titterington (2001) pointed out that by examining homicide rates alone researchers would draw the conclusion that men are 9 times more likely to commit lethal violence than women; however, when suicide is also included, men are only 5.5 times more likely than women to resort to lethal violence. They further found that while women exhibited a higher suicide-homicide ratio than men, meaning they were more prone to choosing suicide over homicide, men exhibited no such preferences with a suicide-homicide ratio falling between .475 and .568 for each of the 19 years from 1979 to 1997. Finally, through longitudinal analysis, they noted that while trends in the direction of violence did not vary between men and women, trends in the production of violence varied greatly, with men's lethal violence cycling up and down while female violence continuously decreased between 1979 and 1997. Based on their results, Vollum and Titterington asserted that the integrated model provides a clearer picture of gender differences, both in the volume of lethality (which they see as underestimated in studies that examine homicide alone) and the direction of lethality (which appears to be structured differently and to trend differently for women).

Building on Vollum and Titterington's research, Batton (2004) further examined the gender differences in self-directed and other-directed lethal violence rates over time in the United States from 1960 to 2000. She found evidence of a consistently higher suicide-homicide ratio for women than men throughout the time frame of her study. In contrast to Vollum and Titterington, however, Batton found similar trends in changes over time for both the male and female suicide-homicide ratio, a finding which she admits is likely to be the result of sample differences in the two studies. Recognizing that women's societal roles have changed significantly in recent decades, Batton hypothesized that female labor force participation should play a role in both lethal violence rates and suicide-homicide ratios for women. She further hypothesized that divorce rates, economic conditions, U.S. military engagements and alcohol consumption should play significant roles in explaining gender differences in the suicide-homicide ratio over time. Applying seemingly unrelated regression techniques, Batton found evidence of a positive relationship between alcohol consumption rates, sex-specific unemployment rates and involvement in foreign wars and the lethal violence rate for both men and women. She further found the percentage of population between 10 and 19 to be negatively correlated with male and female lethal violence rates. She also found extent of female labor force participation to be negatively correlated to female lethal violence only, and the business failure rate to be negatively correlated to male lethal violence only. Batton's analysis of the suicide-homicide ratio revealed a negative correlation with alcohol consumption, family poverty rates, and female labor force participation for both sexes, and a positive correlation for size of the youthful population for both sexes. For Batton, these several hypotheses and her findings are presented within the "contextual framework" of the integrated model, but are also ". . . consistent with other theoretical perspectives, such as general strain theory and institutional-anomic [*sic*] theory" (453).

Responding to a call for more integrated research within the epidemiological literature (see: Mercy, Krug, Dahlberg, and Zwi 2003; Rockett 1998), at least one scholar turned to the integrated model to examine lethal violence as an international public health issue. Citing the importance of regional cultural differences (such as religion), Rezaeian (2008) examined lethal violence rates of four high GNP and 18 low GNP countries located in the Eastern Mediterranean region of the world. Disaggregating the lethal violence rate by age and gender, he reported only descriptive statistics on the suicide-homicide ratio, which appeared to be elevated for males in low and middle income countries as opposed to those in high income countries. He found the opposite for females, but without any measures of statistical significance; given the small sample size of only 4 high GNP countries, it is difficult to infer much from these particular findings. Unfortunately, Rezaeian provided little theoretical justification for his application of the integrated model. He did, however, provide a brief account of how important regional cultural differences can be in understanding the suicide-homicide ratio. In a later study, Rezaeian (2011) expanded his previous analysis of the Eastern Mediterranean region to include data on each of the six world regions identified by the United Nations. From this expanded study he identified three distinct regional categories:

> 1. The first group, which includes Southeast Asia, Europe, and Western Pacific, is the group in which lethal violence in both males and females directs inward in the form of suicide. . . .
> 2. The second group, which includes only Africa, is the group in which lethal violence in both males and females directs outward in the form of homicide.

> 3. Finally, the third group, which includes America and Eastern Mediterranean, is rather a mix [sic] group. In both regions and in males (except 60 years and older in America) lethal violence directs outward in the form of homicide whereas in females it directs inward in the form of suicide. . . . (2011:5)

Unfortunately, as discussed above, this partial application of the integrated model is of only limited utility. Even though Rezaeian found some support for the integrated model, because he ignored forces of production it is unclear how to interpret his cross-national findings. Rezaeian did, however, raise an important issue by questioning the value of international studies in identifying the effects of cultural variables that may be heavily influenced by regional cultural practices. Consequently, Rezaeian suggested that future research should focus on significantly smaller units of analysis.

Recently, Lanier (2010) employed the integrated model to examine the incidence of lethal violence among American Indians. She argued that the integrated model's focus on both structural and cultural conditions makes it uniquely suited for testing the social conditions generated by the historical experiences of ". . . colonization, forced assimilation, and oppression. . . " (p. 84) that have shaped modern American Indian life. Lanier found a significant positive correlation between percentage of American Indian female-headed households and an economic index (consisting of percentage of American Indians living in poverty and percent unemployed) with the lethal violence rate. She also found the suicide-homicide ratio to be negatively correlated with percentage of American Indian female-headed households, which she interpreted as a ". . . break down in the strength of the relational system. . . " (p. 83) that in turn led to an externalization of blame.

Together, these five studies provide evidence of the integrated model's potential for providing a clearer understanding of the lethal violence rate and its individual components of homicide and suicide. Unfortunately, several of these studies provided weak justification for the application of the integrated model to their particular area of intrest and failed to fully utilize the model by only focusing on the suicide-homicide ratio without including total lethal violence rate. These shortcomings also appear in the scholarship testing the integrated model.

Testing the Integrated Model

Over the past decade, several scholars have either attempted to replicate Unnithan et al.'s findings, or they attempted to test portions of the integrated model. Several of these studies fall short of testing the model by focusing only on the suicide-homicide ratio and failing to take forces of production into account, while other studies focused primarily on replicating the result of Unnithan et al.'s original findings with different data sources.

Fernquist (2002) conducted the first test of the integrated model by examining age-standardized male and female suicide and homicide rates in 21 developed nations to determine if either the lethal violence rate or the suicide-homicide proportion provide more explanatory power than the disaggregated rates (Fernquist argued that the suicide-homicide ratio is actually a proportion which he abbreviates as SHP). Based on his analysis of divorce rates, female labor force participation rates, fertility rates, annual percentage of all religious books published, Gini index, GDP, and collectivism, he concluded:

> . . . that instead of examining LVR, researchers would do better to examine suicide and homicide rates separately. The reasons cross-national research on LVR is [*sic*] not needed are: (1) the rank-order of suicide and homicide in the 21 developed countries is very dissimilar; (2) suicide and homicide are weakly correlated; (3) coefficients from the MGLS LVR models add basically no new substantive information compared to suicide models. (P. 245)

Fernquist went on to note that "research on SHP, however, does offer unique insights into how suicide and homicide rates are impacted by the same independent variables" (245). While this may initially appear to be compelling evidence against the integrated model, Unnithan et al. themselves admitted that, although there is no information contained in the LVR that is not already in the suicide and homicide rates individually, the significance of the integrated model lies in its ability to ferret out which variables are truly forces of production from those that only appear to be forces of production when measured in incomplete, disaggregated models.

Further probing the value of the integrated model, He, Cao, Wells and Maguire (2003) resurrected one of Henry and Short's suggested hypotheses for future research. In particular, they examined international data to determine if divorce rates were negatively correlated with homicide rates and positively correlated with suicide rates. They offered two critiques of data used in Unnithan et al.'s initial test of the integrated model. First, they noted that the cross-sectional selection of countries included data points spread out over a 20-year period. Second, they criticized Unnithan et al.'s failure to include key variables identified by Henry and Short as central to the frustration-aggression hypothesis. To rectify these concerns, and to incorporate findings by Lester and Yang (1998) on the unemployment rate's influence on lethal violence, He and his colleagues retested the integrated model using cross-sectional international data from 64 countries which had reported suicide and homicide rates at least once between 1989 and 1993. For independent variables, they included divorce rates, unemployment rates, the Gini index (which they claim is a better measure of inequality than income share of the highest quintile), and GNP. Their analysis confirmed Unnithan et al.'s prior findings by clearly demonstrating that increases in income inequality channel lethal violence outward while higher levels of economic development channel lethal violence internally. Moreover, neither measure held a significant influence on the lethal violence rate. The inclusion of divorce rates, however, does not support Henry and Short's hypothesis, as He et al. only found a significant relationship between divorce rates and the overall lethal violence rate but not the suicide-homicide ratio. Finally, they found no evidence of a significant relationship between unemployment rates and either the lethal violence rate or the suicide-homicide ratio.

While Unnithan et al. successfully used the integrated model to demonstrate how individually examining homicide or suicide can lead to misidentifying a force of direction as a force of production or vice versa, Wu (2003) set out to test the integrated model by predicting from theory, prior to running his models, which variables would act as forces of direction and which would act as forces of production. Identifying commonly accepted measures of structural inequality, he hypothesized that poverty, the Gini index, teen mothers, unemployment, infant mortality and the percentage of non-white residents would each be positively correlated with the lethal violence rate of U.S. counties with populations over 100,000. Wu then identified five indicators of attribution: immigration, which he linked with external blame since it challenges existing community norms; residential racial segregation, which can foster us-versus-them mentalities; divorce, which he tied to higher rates of self-blame; and college educated residents and professional work force participation, which he linked to higher levels of personal responsibility. Employing OLS regressions, Wu confirmed each of his hypotheses predicting the forces of production; however, he was only able to confirm one of his hypotheses about force of direction (i.e., segregation is negatively correlated with the suicide-homicide ratio.) Interestingly, Wu did find significant negative correlations between several of his forces of production (i.e., unemployment rate, Gini index, infant mortality rate and percent non-white) and the suicide-homicide ratio. Moreover, Wu also found a significant negative relationship between a control variable measuring whether or not a county was located in the South and the suicide-homicide ratio. Overall, Wu claimed these findings clearly demonstrate the interwoven nature of the causes of homicide and suicide, making the focus on lethal violence a useful way of identifying where policy decisions may gain the most ground. However, he cautioned that future research needs to be very clear about theorizing and conceptualizing forces of direction.

In another incomplete test of the integrated model, Wu (2004) tested Unnithan et al.'s attribution hypothesis against two competing theories of how suicide or homicide might result from social deprivation. As with his earlier research, Wu identified residential racial segregation and immigration as two measures of external attribution, along with the Gini index. Although he found no significant relationship between the Gini index and the suicide-homicide ratio in counties with populations larger than 100,000, he did find support for the integrated model's attribution hypothesis by demonstrating that the immigration rate and the segregation index are both negatively correlated with the suicide-homicide ratio. While Wu found support for the integrated model, his analysis was primarily a test of the attribution hypothesis rather than stream theory as a whole.

In yet another example of a partial test of the integrated model, Bills and Li (2005) measured the strength of the relationship between age-adjusted homicide and suicide rates in 65 countries. They found no evidence of a correlation between homicide and suicide in their data as a whole, but they did find significant relationships between the two forms of lethal violence in some of their regional models. In particular, they found a positive correlation in Europe and negative correlation in Asia Pacific and the Americas. They pointed out that in this regard:

> . . . in looking at the degree of difference and diversity among the countries selected, the lack of a strong correlation between rates of homicide and suicide is not surprising. . . . Although such findings do not provide evidence for a strong correlation between homicide and suicide rates, they do not necessarily negate the possibility that a significant relationship does exist in certain geographic regions . . . . (P. 841)

In fact, Bills and Li further suggested that, given the importance of cultural conditions in the theoretical underpinnings of the integrated model, it is no surprise that their models showed stronger results at the regional level. They further claimed that their results indicated that regional differences may play a more central role in the suicide-homicide ratio than either gender differences or economic measures. Moreover, their findings seem to indicate that smaller geographical units of analysis may provide clearer results by reducing the degree of heterogeneity of cultural influences on types of attribution.

In the most recent test of Unnithan et al.'s integrated model, Chon (2013) examined the homicide rates, suicide rates and lethal violence rates of 124 nations. Chon identified several variables that he expected to affect the suicide-homicide ratio, including age, gender income inequality, and proximity to the former communist bloc. Chon discussed age, in particular the influence of a large elderly population, at great length, arguing that factors ranging from social isolation to lower levels of self-concept all increase the elderly's risk for internal attribution. Similarly, he argued that gender is important, as men's self-concept is tied to their jobs and therefore their economic security, consequently leading him to predict higher levels of internal attribution from men. As with earlier tests of the integrated model, Chon also included several measures of economic inequality as a factor that should lead to external attribution of blame. Finally, he included membership in the former communist bloc as a predictor of internal attribution of blame, which he indicated could be linked to a number of factors including high rates of alcoholism, the anomic nature of the collapse of communism, or high rates of atheism.

Examining homicide by itself, Chon found a significant negative relationship of homicide rates with both GDP and percent of population over 65, and a significant positive relationship between the Gini index and homicide rates. Turning to suicide by itself, Chon found no significant relationships between any of the measures and the suicide rate. When analyzing the integrated model, Chon found no significant statistical relationship between any of the variables and the lethal violence rate; however, he did find that GDP and percent of the population over 65 were both significantly and positively correlated with the suicide-homicide ratio, while the Gini index was significantly and negatively correlated with the suicide-homicide ratio. These findings provide support for the integrated model, inasmuch as they demonstrate how researchers measuring homicide and suicide separately might mistake variables such as GDP, percent elderly and the Gini index as forces that reduce or increase homicide rates with no effect on suicide rates, when in reality these variables are acting as forces of direction between homicide and suicide rather than as forces of production for homicide.

Revising the Integrated Model

Predominantly in response to Wu's (2003; 2004) concern that the theoretical underpinnings of the suicide-homicide ratio are unclear, several scholars began to develop modified versions of the integrated model that merge its framework with other classical theories. Both social learning theory and Durkheim's integration/regulation theory have been proposed as alternatives to Unnithan et al.'s micro-psychologically based explanations of forces of direction and production.

Batton and Ogle (2003) attempted to merge social learning theory with the integrated model in order to clarify forces of direction. Pointing out that attribution styles emerge from social learning processes, they hypothesized that because of gender differences in attribution styles and norms governing the experience and expression of aggression, females are more likely to internalize aggression while males are more likely to externalize aggression. Batton and Ogle then tested this hypothesis by examining male and female suicide-homicide ratios in the United States for the period 1963 to 1998. Furthermore, Batton and Ogle employed social learning theory to predict and confirm lower suicide-homicide ratios for African Americans, driven by social inequalities, that lead to external blaming among minorities in America. In their last analysis, Batton and Ogle returned to the question of regional differences and found that:

> . . . the average SHR values for the Confederate South were .50 (1982) and .42 (1997) and were similar for the Census South at .53 (1982) and .42 (1997). These figures are lower than those for the non-South, which were .69 for both 1982 and 1997 indicating a greater proportion of suicidal relative to homicidal violence. (P. 101)

Batton and Ogle admitted that while none of these findings empirically tests the integrated model itself, the findings did lend credence to the idea that social learning theory may be one avenue through which differences in attribution could be better understood.

O'Brien and Stockard (2006) modified Unnithan et al.'s theory by shifting away from the micro-psychological, Freudian-influenced aggression/frustration hypothesis toward a more macro-sociological, Durkheimian perspective. Building from Durkheim, O'Brien and Stockard hypothesized:

> . . . that insufficient social integration/regulation is a "force of production" that increases both suicide and homicide. This view differs from Durkheim who saw lack of regulation as a "force of production" for both suicide and homicide, but viewed a lack of integration as increasing suicide and decreasing homicide in modern societies. (P. 1552-1553)

To test the usefulness of the integrated model, they examined the effects of non-marital births and relative cohort size on suicide, homicide, and the residuals for homicide and suicide for men and women as well as blacks and whites in the United States for the period 1930 to 2000. They concluded that shifts in the age distribution for homicide and suicide rates between 1930 and 2000 are related, and that more than half the variance in these shifts can be explained by non-marital births and relative cohort size.

Furthermore, they concluded that replacing the frustration element of the integrated model with a modified version of Durkheim's social integration/regulation can produce significant results in identifying forces of production. This approach of incorporating Durkheim's theories into the integrated model is also supported by Batton's (2004) claim that an alternative explanation consistent with her findings could be found in anomie theory. Moreover, O'Brien and Stockard's approach provides the fundamental groundwork for a macro-sociological explanation of forces of production that relies on measures of community integration and regulation as opposed to the micro-psychological measures of individual frustration.

SUMMARY AND CONCLUSIONS

Inventory of Empirical Findings

The most interesting conclusion to be drawn from the studies cited above is the generally consistent validation of the integrated model's investigative value. With the exception of the few partial tests of the model, most researchers have found the integrated model's approach useful in teasing out the connections between homicide and suicide. Also important is that, given the spatial and temporal influence on cultural variables, cross-sectional studies that focus on smaller units of analysis may be preferred to international longitudinal research when identifying cultural influences on the suicide-homicide ratio. Previous research has explored a wide range of variables potentially related to lethal violence, including gender, economic inequalities, race, immigration, region, divorce, female labor-force participation and age at a number of different levels of analysis, including global regions, countries, U.S. states and counties.

Gaps in the Research Literature

Despite the breadth of variables that have been examined in the context of the integrated model, *religion*, one key variable in suicide research and one of recent interest in homicide studies, has been thus far ignored. Moreover, there are only a limited number of complete tests of the integrated model, and those focus predominantly on the variables drawn from the original formulation. Given the synergistic nature of the model, it becomes fruitless to attempt partial tests, especially those that focus solely on the suicide-homicide ratio, since this measure is highly dependent on the lethal violence rate itself. Perhaps the most common and egregious error found throughout the lethal violence literature hinges around the misconception that partial tests of the integrated model are feasible. This limited interpretation of the stream theory began with Durkheim, and can be seen in the literature up until the late 1990s when Lester and Yang make a similar assumption. Consequently, research that underscores the value of identifying both forces of production and forces of direction and further examines the interaction between these two concepts is badly needed.

It is also important to consider the vague handling of the theoretical underpinnings of forces of direction and forces of production in the original statement of the integrated model. As Wu (2003; 2004) cogently notes, research set within the integrated framework must carefully identify the theoretical justifications for expecting any variable to operate as either a force of production or as a force of direction. Finally, while some scholars have made progress in explicating the macro-sociological processes underlying forces of production, no progress has been made toward a more macro-sociological understanding of forces of direction; this is something Unnithan et al. suggest is badly needed for the future development of the integrated model.

The Need to Incorporate Religion

Given the heavy cultural and regional influence on suicide-homicide ratios, noted in the literature, several researchers have suggested that future studies investigate religious implications (Chon 2013; Rezaeian 2008; Rezaeian 2011). Unnithan et al. even relied partly on religious differences between evangelicals and mainline Protestants to develop their argument for why the suicide-homicide ratio would respond as it does to regional measures in the United States. Furthermore, religion has served as a benchmark variable within the suicide literature over the past century (e.g., Durkheim [1897] 1979; Faupel, Kowalski, and Starr 1987; Gearing and Lizardi 2009; Stack 2000b; Wray, Colen, and Pescosolido 2011); is becoming increasingly one of interest within the criminology literature (e.g., Akers 2010; Cullen 2010; Desmond, Kikuchi, and Morgan 2010; DiIulio 2009; Johnson and Jang 2010); and is also beginning to appear within the public health literature on lethal violence (e.g., Gearing and Lizardi 2009; Hummer, Ellision, Rogers, Moulton, and Romero 2004; Mercy, Krug, Dahlberg, and Zwi 2003).

Moreover, developing a test of the complete integrated model with a central focus on religion will serve several important purposes: (1) it will provide a thorough test of the integrated model that goes beyond its original focus on economic and regional variables; (2) it will examine in detail the complex interactions between community religiosity and denominational composition of communities; and, (3) it will offer an opportunity to merge the theoretical literature examining religion's role in suicide and homicide.

CHAPTER 3:

Religion and Lethal Violence Rates

This chapter examines the theoretical and empirical connections between religion and lethal violence rates in the United States. The first section draws a distinction between theories focusing on religion as a social institution and theories focusing on differences among religious denominations. The second section traces the historical development of the institutional effects literature which links the overall religiosity of a community with the susceptibility of its members to antisocial behavior. The third section explores the literature on denominational effects of religious congregations on community homicide and suicide rates. The fourth and final section of this chapter evaluates the larger picture by addressing the integrated model's ability to incorporate both institutional and denominational effects of religion into a single framework capable of explaining their respective influences on lethal violence rates.

INSTITUTIONAL VERSUS DENOMINATIONAL EFFECTS

Within the macro-sociological and macro-criminological literature pertaining to religion and antisocial behavior, a clear divide can be drawn between scholarship focused on religion's institutional effects and scholarship focused on religion's denominational effects. Scholars focusing on the institutional effects suggest that local communities characterized by large numbers of church attendees (Bainbridge 1989; Breault 1986; Stack 1983; Stark, Doyle, and Rushing 1983), high frequencies of church attendance (Stark 1996), or churches per capita (Lee 2006; Walker 2009) should experience lower rates of antisocial behavior due to the pervasive influence of religion's normative structure on everyday life for these communities (Stark and Bainbridge

1996; Stark, Kent, and Doyle 1982). In contrast, research and scholarship on denominational effects, popularized in sociology principally by Durkheim, suggests that differences in culture and social structure between religious groups should result in different impacts on antisocial behavior such as suicide or homicide. While precious little scholarship exists directly addressing the differences in these two approaches, Stark and Bainbridge (1996) argue persuasively that there are important differences in what these two approaches measure that carry with them the potential for different effects on behavior. They note in this regard:

> . . . since all these religious bodies foster moral teachings incompatible with delinquent behavior, variations in delinquency by denomination ought not reflect theological differences, but primarily differences in the proportion of highly committed members each group manages to maintain. That is, Episcopalians differ from Baptists not so much in what the respective churches want from their members as in the degree to which they successfully engender high levels of commitment. (P. 71)

One of the advantages of the integrated model is that it provides an effective means for bringing both of these literatures together by analyzing the institutional effects of community religiosity as forces of production and the denominational effects as forces of inward or outward direction.

RELIGION'S INSTITUTIONAL EFFECTS

Historical Development. Throughout the 1970s and 1980s, a series of debates flared up around the controversial findings of Travis Hirschi and Rodney Stark set forth in their 1969 paper "Hellfire and Delinquency." Deeply influenced by social control theory, Hirschi and Stark hypothesized that juveniles who believe in a punitive afterlife should be less likely to engage in deviant acts than their less religious peers who believe they have nothing to fear from the hereafter. Focusing their attention on 4,077 students enrolled in public middle and high schools in Western Contra Costa County in California, Hirschi and Stark operationalized belief in the existence of hell through a measure of church attendance and deviant behavior through a scale generated from answers to self-reported behavior about theft, vandalism and assault. Surprisingly, they found no connection within their sample between church attendance and delinquent behavior, a finding that led them to claim that "The church is irrelevant to delinquency because it fails to instill in its members love for their neighbors and because belief in the possibility of pleasure and pain in another world cannot now, and perhaps never could, compete with the pleasures and pains of everyday life" (Hirschi and Stark 1969:212-213). In general, this dire conclusion and the data supporting it were met over the next two decades with a number of studies touting contrary results and several attempts were made at theoretical modifications to reconcile these mixed findings being reported in the literature.

Perhaps the first and most straightforward attempt to salvage Hirschi and Stark's "hellfire hypothesis" came from Burkett and White (1974), who argued that religion's pressure to abstain from deviant behavior may only be accurately measured when the deviance in question is relatively minor. They asserted that religion's ability to reduce delinquent behavior may be difficult to pinpoint since other major institutions similarly frown upon antisocial behavior. Consequently, they suggested that religion's protective effects should be easier to identify in studies focused on aesthetic prohibitions more unique to religion rather than violations of major social mores. To test this hypothesis, Burkett and White surveyed 855 high school seniors from three Pacific Northwest high schools, replicating Hirschi and Stark's study with the addition of self-reported rates of alcohol and marijuana use as measures of minor forms of delinquency. They found a weak negative correlation between church attendance and self-reported incidents of crime (i.e. larceny, vandalism and assault), and a much stronger negative correlation between church attendance and frequency of alcohol and marijuana consumption. While they did find evidence for their anti-aesthetic hypothesis, and also replicated the results from Hirschi and Stark's previous study with a different sample, it is important to note that neither of these widely-read studies examined any form of violence more serious than simple assaults.

Attempting to further replicate Hirschi and Stark's and Burkett and White's results, a number of studies carried out throughout the United States began to report widely divergent findings. First, Albrecht,

Chadwick and Alcorn (1977) found evidence of a negative correlation between religious participation and deviant behavior (i.e., smoking cigarettes, consuming alcohol, smoking marijuana, taking drugs, premarital sex, theft, and assault) among 244 teenagers living in predominantly Mormon communities in Utah, Idaho and Los Angeles, California. They attributed this finding to two factors -- namely their inclusion of measures of peer behavior and family relationships, and the religious salience of their sample occasioned by their focus on highly religious Mormon wards. Higgins and Albrecht (1977), however, reached a different conclusion after attempting to replicate Hirschi and Stark's study with 1,383 high school sophomores in Atlanta, Georgia. They found church attendance to have a moderate to strong effect on both minor and serious forms of deviant behavior, findings which they argued may be attributed to regional differences between the West and South in the United States. In particular, Higgins and Albrecht speculated that church attendance in the South may reflect stronger commitments to religious ideals than church attendance in the West.

Moral communities and institutional strength. Given these divergent findings and varied conclusions, Stark, Kent and Doyle (1982) attempted to clarify these numerous inconsistencies by reconceptualizing religion's relationship with deviant behavior. Specifically, they pointed to the previous research's focus on individuals and their relationship with religion as being too limited. Instead, they insisted that cultural and structural religious factors come into play to determine whether or not an individuals' religious participation influences their day-to-day decision making. In short, Stark et al. argued that highly secular communities, such as those found on the Pacific coast, will provide little routine pressure for individuals to conform to their religious beliefs. In stark contrast, communities consisting of more religious inhabitants (virtually everywhere in the United States except the Pacific west, by Stark et al.'s definition) will act as functional 'moral communities' that continuously remind their members (believers and nonbelievers alike) of religious beliefs and obligations. To test this "moral communities hypothesis", Stark et al. gathered data on delinquency and church attendance for 1,213 teens in Seattle, Washington, which they successfully used to replicate Hirschi and Stark's original findings. Next, they analyzed a national data set of tenth grade boys to demonstrate the negative correlation between religious participation and delinquency in communities throughout the rest of the United States. Stark and Bainbridge (1996), in their book entitled *Religion, Deviance, and Social Control*, explained how the moral communities theory bridges the gap between earlier inconsistent individual-level findings by shifting from individual religiosity to community religiosity:

> We suggest that what counts is not only whether a particular person is religious, but whether this religiousness is or is not ratified by the social environment. The idea here is that religion is empowered to produce conformity to the norms only as it is sustained through interaction and accepted by the majority as a valid basis for action. (P. 72)

Expanding beyond the social control foundations of the moral communities hypothesis, Lee (2006) argued that strong religious institutions reduce community violence by "facilitating networks, transmitting norms, and fostering community." Examining 902 rural counties, he found evidence to support the notion that moral communities (measured as religious adherence rate) and the institutional strength of religion (measured as churches per 1,000 residents) reduce the violent crime rate. Lee also found the violent crime rate to be positively correlated with population turnover, percent conservative/evangelical Protestant, and general inequality, as well as negatively correlated with ethnic homogeneity and the percent of religious adherents belonging to civically-engaged churches.

Unfortunately, it is difficult to draw conclusions from much of the previous literature examining the influence of religiosity on antisocial behavior either at the micro or macro level because the field is rife with methodological differences in study design, sampling methods and population choices (Baier and Wright 2001; Hoffmann and Bahr 2006; Johnson, De Li, Larson, and McCullough 2000; Knudten and Knudten 1971). Another concern is that prior research has tended toward analyzing religion's influence on adolescents only (Hoffmann and Bahr 2006). Among other limitations of prior research on religion's institutional effects are a general absence of empirical examinations of macro-level data (Johnson and Jang 2010) and a tendency to focus on non-lethal violence, such as assault (e.g., Cretacci 2003; Pearce and

Haynie 2004; Sloane and Potvin 1986; Tittle and Welch 1983), or robbery (e.g., Benda and Corwyn 1997; Benda and Toombs 2000; Elifson, Petersen, and Hadaway 1983; Evans, Cullen, Dunaway, and Burton 1995). Despite the limitations of the current empirical research, it is nonetheless reasonable to infer an inverse relationship between measures of religious institutional strength and either homicide or suicide. In particular, each of the above theoretical approaches would predict lower homicide rates and lower suicide rates in communities with stronger religious institutions.

Burkett and White's anti-aesthetic hypothesis raises three relevant issues. First, existing research confirming this theory has been limited to relatively minor acts of violence such as simple assault. Second, the hypothesis does not claim that religion holds no influence on serious antisocial behavior but, rather, that the influence is difficult to detect given the influence of other social institutions. Consequently, testing the influence of religion on lethal violence will require close attention to control variables that take other social institutions (e.g., family) into account. Finally, it is important to remember that the anti-aesthetic hypothesis only addresses the difficulty in measuring religion's ability to transmit norms. It does not, however, address religion's ability to facilitate interpersonal networks and foster a sense of community, either or both of which may play stronger roles in reducing antisocial behavior than do normative prohibitions (see Robins and Fiske 2009).

It is also worth noting the diversity of ways in which religious institutional strength has previously been conceptualized. Most scholars have focused on the proportion of religious participants in the community as a measure of religions influence over the community as a whole, which Stark and Bainbridge (1996) suggest captures religion's ability "to produce conformity to the norms only as it is sustained through interaction and accepted by the majority as a valid basis for action" (72). Lee (2006), however, focuses on a separate dimension by examining the prevalence of churches within a community as an indicator of religion's institutional strength, which he contends ". . . focuses on the concrete role social institutions play in structuring social interaction, facilitating networks, transmitting norms, and fostering community" (314). A third, and perhaps equally important concept is that of religious homogeneity, which Ellison, Burr and McCall (1997) suggest should play a role in further amplifying the effects of religious institutions by sustaining ". . . a sense of local tradition and identity, and a coherent narrative of community life that links residents across generations and social classes" (277). While all three of these conceptualizations have never been tested within the same study, it seems that each one individually has the potential to contribute to our understanding of the strength of religious institutions with respect to shaping behavior.

RELIGION'S DENOMINATIONAL EFFECTS

In the early days of sociological thought, in his treatise on suicide, Durkheim ([1897] 1979) steered much of the future research on religious effects toward a study of denominational effects; this entailed focusing on the differences between Protestant and Catholic communities. Durkheim theorized that Protestants and Catholics produced different levels of social integration throughout the communities that they occupied. On the one hand, Protestants' theological focus on the individual's salvation and connection with God led to weaker social integration, as social norms espoused by the Protestant churches encouraged an individualistic outlook throughout the community. In contrast, Catholics placed far more importance on the functions of the church for salvation and the interdependence between the individual and the religious community. Consequently, the Catholic Church fostered strong integration throughout the community. For Durkheim, this difference in levels of integration explains the higher rates of suicide among Protestant countries than Catholic ones, as the weaker levels of integration within Protestant countries provides less protection from self-destructive behavior.

Social networks and suicide. One of the more prominent attempts to update and refine Durkheim's theory of denominational effects is provided by Pescosolido and Georgianna (1989), and further developed by Pescosolido (1990; 1994) in later work. Their approach to Durkheim's legacy begins by questioning the wisdom of continuing to use percent Protestant and percent Catholic as measures of social integration given the cultural differences between 19th century Europe and 20th century America. Having raised concerns about the overreliance on Durkheim's original operationalization of social integration in modern research, Pescosolido and Georgianna noted the difficulty in identifying alternative measures given the vague nature of

Durkheim's conceptualization of social integration. Consequently, they suggested that by reconceptualizing both social integration and social regulation as functions of social networks, the interdependent nature of Durkheim's core concepts becomes clearer and the stage is set for identifying which modern religious denominations best represent balanced social networks that do not over or under produce regulation or integration.

The main contribution of their approach is found in their having identified the specific mechanisms behind two of Durkheim's key concepts. As Pescosolido explains, ". . . proposing the social mechanism behind Durkheim's general concepts of integration and regulation provides a more concrete hold on how to tailor old hypotheses to new sociocultural locations and to derive new propositions and hypotheses from Durkheim's general theory" (1994:267). To this end, Pescosolido and Georgianna introduced a social network framework from which to recast Durkheim's ideas. In doing so, they argued that they are better able to explain the relationship between religion and both integration and regulation by identifying the influence of social network properties, of various denominations, on community suicide rates. Within this theoretical framework, Pescosolido (1994) restated Durkheim's core ideas as follows:

> Durkheim's theoretical scheme can be imagined in a network perspective. In its most basic form, social structure is a safety net that has different features topographically, one dimension running from left to right represents integration; underintegration is represented by sparse network ties and overintegration by dense or strong network ties. Another dimension, running forward to back and representing regulation, similarly runs from dense to sparse in terms of network ties. When these two are considered simultaneously, the clarity provided by this network depiction is, in itself, useful. When individuals exist in social structures with either too little integration or regulation, the social safety net is "loose" or "open," there is little to "catch" individuals when crisis destabilizes their equilibrium. They fall through the net, and suicides occur....When individuals exist in social structures which are too regulated or too integrated, the safety

> net closes up. There is no flexibility or "give" to the social safety net. When they experience crisis, in essence they hit a wall which shatters rather than supports. It is only in the center of the net, where social networks are balanced and moderate in their provision of integration and/or regulation, in which individuals can be safely "caught" and restrained from their suicidal impulses. (P. 276)

Pescosolido went on to explain that this approach further clarifies the relationship between the micro and macro processes by providing a theoretical framework in which social interaction can be viewed as the key focus at any level of analysis. Pescosolido argued that social networks bridge the chasm between micro and macro sociological thought by focusing on social interaction, whether it occurs between two individuals or members of a large community.

She further argued that Durkheim's understanding of religious differences between Protestants and Catholics is limited to his specific geopolitical time period. She pointed out that: "In the contemporary U.S., three sociohistorial trends (secularization, ecumenicalism in the 1960s, and the post-World War II evangelical revival) realigned the relationship among Protestant denominations, Catholicism and Judaism" (p. 271). She further noted that these changes have created two distinct branches of Protestantism: mainline Protestants and evangelical Protestants, the latter of which resemble Durkheim's Protestants in their style of social interaction while the former interact in ways more consistent with Catholic congregations. Consequently, Pescosolido and Georgianna suggested that treating Protestants as a homogenous group vastly underestimates the variance in levels of integration among Protestants in modern American society. To test these ideas, Pescosolido and Georgianna (1989) examined county-level suicide statistics for 1970 and found that ". . . Protestant denominations whose presence increased the county group's suicides are mostly 'mainline,' 'mainstream,' or 'old-line' . . ." (p. 38). Furthermore, they found that ". . . Protestant denominations whose presence exert the most protective influences are mostly evangelical . . . " (p. 39).

Social networks and homicide. Roughly a decade after Pescosolido and Georgianna's revision of Durkheim, a parallel set of ideas began appearing in the homicide literature. First, Lee and Bartkowski (2004a;

2004b) suggested a link between the level of civic engagement generated by particular religious denominations and county lethal homicide rates. Then, Beyerlein and Hipp (2005) proposed that the influence of religious denominations on homicide rates depends on whether or not they foster bridging or bonding social networks.

Paralleling Pescosolido and Georgianna's work, Lee and Bartkowski (2004a) recast several major macro-theoretical perspectives in the field of homicide research into a social capital framework.

> Although the concentrated disadvantage and strain perspectives are typically viewed as analytically separate, they have at least one important affinity: They both suggest crime rates are primarily driven by a process of normative breakdown due to deficits in the socialization functions of major social institutions. Whether citing social, familial, economic, religious, or political institutions, these major theories (and others) assume that the institutions so vital to maintaining social order and regulating group behavior patterns are, in one way or another, rendered ineffective. If adapted to integrate the language of social capital, these theories reveal how the networks, norms and trust usually engendered through institutional participation and attachment (i.e., aggregate social capital) are effectively weakened, thus causing crime rates to increase. (P. 9-10)

Lee and Bartkowski further conceptualized the key mechanism behind social capital as civic participation. They argued that civic participation acts both as a source of normative socialization and as a catalyst for strengthening social networks. Drawing a distinction between 'open' (available to any age group) and 'closed' (limited to particular age groups) social networks, they focused on religion as an example of the former and voting as an example of the latter. They hypothesized that the open networks of religious groups should protect communities from homicide irrespective of their age structure, while the closed networks produced by political participation should only provide protective benefits to communities with disproportionately older populations. Lee and Bartkowski tested their hypotheses with county-level data examining the protective effects of the proportion of adherents to civically-engaged denominations, the number of churches per 100,000 residents, the voter turnout rate for presidential elections, and the number of social/civic organizations per 100,000 residents on juvenile and adult homicide rates. Employing negative binomial regressions, they found the juvenile homicide rates to be significantly and negatively correlated with religious civic participation and significantly positively correlated with several of their control variables, including juvenile population size, divorce rate, percent black, and concentrated poverty. Adult homicide rates, however, were found to be negatively correlated with both religious and secular civic participation. Furthermore, they found all of their control variables to be significantly correlated with adult homicide rates (negative: aged 15 to 29; positive: adult population size, divorce rate, percent black, concentrated poverty, South, and West). Lee and Bartkowski concluded that civically-engaged religious denominations provide a strong protective effect from homicide for all members of the community by fostering open social networks that strengthen the entire community.

Further refining the theoretical linkage between social networks and homicide rates, Beyerlein and Hipp (2005) pointed to two types of social capital initially identified by Putnam in his classic work on types of social capital: "Bonding social capital consists of network structures in which connections are primarily or entirely among members of the same group, while bridging social capital consists of network structures in which connections crosscut members of different groups" (996). They then made the case that these two forms of social capital may produce radically different homicide rates. Since bridging social capital provides broader social networks than bonding social capital, the former would be more effective at contributing to community-wide social integration, and providing rapid dissemination of norms throughout the community, while groups based on bonding social capital will be more disconnected from the community at large and ultimately provide a barrier to important community functions. To test these hypotheses, Beyerlein and Hipp examined the influence of the proportion of mainline Protestant adherents (to represent bridging social capital) and evangelical Protestant adherents (to represent bonding social capital) on county-level homicide rates. They found a significant positive relationship between the homicide rate and both the proportion of evangelicals and the number of evangelical congregations per 100,000 population. They also found a significant negative correlation between the homicide rate and the proportion of mainline

Protestants and the number of Catholic churches per 100,000 population. Beyerlein and Hipp concluded that the bridging social capital generated in mainline Protestant communities helps to reduce homicide and other crimes by cultivating broad social networks that allow the community to effectively resist crime. On the other hand, the bonding social capital fostered by evangelical Protestants leaves communities unprotected from violent crime as these groups wall themselves off from the larger community and effectively disrupt the community's ability to act collectively against crime.

Two key insights pertaining to religion's influence on lethal violence can be distilled from the denominational effects literature. First, the Protestant population cannot be treated as homogenous; in particular, evangelical Protestants differ from mainline Protestants in important respects, including the nature of the networks they foster and the forms of social capital they generate. Second, the relationship between any given Protestant denomination and lethal violence may vary depending on which form of lethal violence is being examined. Research indicates that the relative presence of evangelicals is negatively correlated with suicide rates (Pescosolido and Georgianna 1989) but positively correlated with homicide rates (Beyerlein and Hipp 2005).

Given the independent trajectories along which the suicide denominational effects and the homicide denominational effects literature has developed, it is no surprise that some inconsistencies have appeared between these two approaches. One particular curiosity is the divergent conclusions formed about the influence of religious networks on homicide and suicide rates. Pescosolido and Georgianna (1989) argue that suicide rates should be lower in evangelical communities than in mainline Protestant communities, given that mainlines provide looser social networks which fail to provide appropriate levels of integrative and regulative force for the community at large. Beyerlein and Hipp (2005), in contrast, argue that homicide rates should be higher in evangelical Protestant communities given that they foster denser social networks which limit integration and regulation with the community at large.

APPLYING THE INTEGRATED MODEL

As the previous chapter demonstrated, one of the advantages of the integrated model is its ability to reveal the bigger picture that can often be obscured in studies based on homicide-centric or suicide-centric approaches. By applying the insights of the integrated model to the existing literature on religion and the individual forms of lethal violence, it is possible to develop a broader set of hypotheses capable of highlighting the potentially complex interrelationships between religion and homicide and suicide rates. The following section will propose three hypothetical models linking different measures of religious structures within communities with levels of lethal violence. The first model focuses on religion's institutional effects. And more specifically, on the protective nature of religion's presence within a community and its influence on the production of lethal violence. The second model shifts attention to denominational effects that potentially direct acts of lethal violence toward suicide or homicide. The third model will then incorporate both institutional and denominational effects into a single integrated model that examines both forces of production and forces of direction. For each model, the implications for suicide rates, homicide rates, overall lethal violence rates, and the suicide-homicide ratio will be explained.

Institutional Effects as Forces of Production

Of the two aforementioned theoretical approaches, those that focus on religion's institutional effects align most closely with the integrated model's forces of production. Researchers following this theoretical reasoning are clearly linking high levels of community religiosity with reductions in antisocial behavior. Since both suicide and homicide are expected to be negatively correlated with community religiosity, it is logical to infer that this religious variable will be negatively correlated with the overall lethal violence rate. In fact, with the exception of the handful of studies focusing on the anti-aesthetic hypothesis, there is good reason to pursue the macro-sociological consequences of religious institutions on lethal violence rates. In particular, religious institutional strength fits into the integrated model framework as a force of production that predicts high lethal violence rates in communities with weaker religious institutional presence. Incorporating the integrated model into the institutional effects literature predicts that strong religious institutions should act as dams that impede the volume of lethal violence that enters the community. In this case, communities with stronger religious institutions should experience lower lethal violence rates for several reasons: (1) religion acts as a deterrent to violence among believers who fear punishment in the afterlife (*hellfire hypothesis*); (2) religion acts as a social control mechanism throughout the community as believers and non-believers alike are discouraged from violent behavior by the religious' context of everyday interactions (*moral communities hypothesis*); (3) religious institutions promote networks and a stronger sense of community (*social capital hypothesis*).

The idea that religion, as an institution, provides protective effects against lethal violence presupposes that levels of formal religious engagement should be negatively correlated with the suicide rate, negatively correlated with the homicide rate, and negatively correlated with the total lethal violence rate. Since this model is focused exclusively on forces of production, it does not provide any theoretical rationale for predicting a relationship between the level of community religiosity and the suicide-homicide ratio. Consequently the following hypotheses can be derived for model #1:

1) Community suicide rates will be inversely correlated with the strength of community religious institutions.
    a. Community suicide rates will be inversely correlated with the proportion of religiously affiliated residents.
    b. Community suicide rates will be inversely correlated with the volume of places of worship within a community.
    c. Community suicide rates will be inversely correlated with the homogeneity of the community's religious population.
2) Community homicide rates will be inversely correlated with the strength of community religious institutions.
    a. Community homicide rates will be inversely correlated with the proportion of religiously affiliated residents.
    b. Community homicide rates will be inversely correlated with the volume of places of worship within a community.
    c. Community homicide rates will be inversely correlated with the homogeneity of the community's religious population.

3) Community lethal violence rates will be inversely correlated with the strength of community religious institutions.
    a. Community lethal violence rates will be inversely correlated with the proportion of religiously affiliated residents.
    b. Community lethal violence rates will be inversely correlated with the volume of places of worship within a community.
    c. Community lethal violence rates will be inversely correlated with the homogeneity of the community's religious population.
4) The suicide-homicide ratio will not be significantly correlated with the strength of community religious intuitions.

Denominational Effects as Forces of Direction

While institutional effects are best conceptualized as forces of production, denominational effects can be conceptualized as potential forces of direction. The theoretical arguments about the differences in the social networks generated by mainline and evangelical denominations imply different relationships for suicide in comparison with homicide. Since both Pescosolido and Georgianna's and Beyerlcin and Hipp's studies divide Protestants into mainline and evangelical, and both identify social networks as the central force behind violence rates, it is reasonable to assume that these social networks are not acting as forces of production since they predict opposite effects on the two types of lethal violence. However, if these denominational differences are acting as forces of direction, then mainline Protestant communities could be effective at reducing homicide and ineffective against suicide, while evangelical communities could be effective at reducing suicide and ineffective against homicide. Within an integrated model approach, evangelical and mainline networks may be acting as forces of direction which in turn play no role in the overall lethal violence rate, but play a pivotal role in determining the suicide-homicide ratio within a community.

In order to better understand the role denominations may play in determining the direction of lethal violence, it is useful to consider both the structural differences (discussed earlier) in how denominations influence community networks as well as the cultural differences in attribution generated by different denominational groups. Prior research on conservative Protestant groups tended to focus on low levels of trust and general acceptance of retributive justice as two cultural attributes that undermined the cohesion of the larger community. Evangelicals, for example, exhibit higher levels of distrust for their neighbors, their coworkers, and even people in general (Mencken, Bader, and Embry 2009). This pervasive and fundamental lack of trust for neighbors and other members of the community can undermine the larger community's efforts to mobilize against and prevent homicides (see: Messner, Baumer, and Rosenfeld 2004; Rosenfeld, Messner, and Baumer 2001; Sampson, Raudenbush, and Earls 1997). Of similar importance to the culture of distrust is a strong affinity toward retributive justice among conservative Protestants. Fundamentalist Protestants, for example, a group that shares conservative roots with evangelicals, have been repeatedly linked to higher levels of retributive beliefs (see Applegate, Cullen, Fisher, and Vander Ven 2000; Grasmick, Davenport, Chamlin, and Bursik 1992). Moreover, research on fundamentalist religious groups has provided evidence that these groups produce higher levels of external attribution of blame throughout their communities by fostering a sense of "us versus them." In this regard, it has been noted that:

> . . . when moral boundaries are rigid, it may be easier to offend or "dis" others and harder to assume a personal responsibility for generating conflict. When there is only good and evil and there has to be a clear moral winner or immoral loser, then the options for controlling violent outcomes may be greatly restricted. (Jensen 2006:9)

Similarly, researchers Ellison, Burr and McCall (2003) hypothesized that high rates of conservative Protestants (a group that also consists of many evangelicals and fundamentalists) might be positively correlated with high rates of homicide due to their acceptance of punitive and vengeful imagery that justifies violence in both self-defense and retaliatory situations, and their commitment to a highly dichotomous morality system. Conversely, the strong bonding networks generated by conservative Protestant communities along with their propensity to view the world in absolute terms of right and wrong should work to insulate the community from suicide by producing tight internally-focused networks while simultaneously shifting the community's attribution of blame externally by adopting a more rigid sense of morality that polarizes these community networks against each other.

In this type of environment, the community becomes inundated with cultural scripts that encourage both distrust of others and a tendency to place blame outside of oneself. Consequently, both the religiously conservative and the non-conservative find themselves at higher risk for homicide because directing frustrations outwardly becomes more likely, and distrust of others undermines the community's ability to police itself. On the other hand, suicide rates would be reduced by the shift away from cultural scripts that call for self-blame and the social support that develops from the tightknit, highly bonded fractions throughout the community.

From these theoretical claims about denominational differences in attribution of blame, it is possible to hypothesize that the larger the presence of denominations that encourage externalization of blame within a community the lower the suicide-homicide ratio. Since this model is based on forces of direction, it in effect assumes a consistent rate of production of lethal violence and, instead, focuses on the likelihood that the violence will manifest as either homicide or suicide. Under this model, it would be expected that denominations that externalize blame would be negatively correlated with suicide rates and positively correlated with homicide rates. Since this model essentially treats the forces of production as exogenous, denominations that externalize blame should have no impact on the total lethal violence rate as increases in homicide should be accompanied by equal decreases in suicide. Consequently, the following hypotheses can be derived for model II:

1) Community suicide rates will be inversely correlated with the proportion of the community that is affiliated with conservative Protestant denominations.
2) Community homicide rates will be positively correlated with the proportion of the community that is affiliated with conservative Protestant denominations.
3) Community lethal violence rates will not be significantly correlated with the proportion of the community that is affiliated with conservative Protestant denominations.

4) Community suicide-homicide ratio will be inversely correlated with the proportion of the community that is affiliated with conservative Protestant denominations.

Institutional/Denominational Conditional Effects Model

This model combines the causal processes of model I and II. As discussed at length in chapter two, both forces of production and forces of direction need to be measured together in order to fully understand the processes involved in lethal violence rates. Consequently, this model encompasses the two dimensions of religious structure under investigation -- namely, religious institutional strength and denominational composition, conceptualizing the former as a force of production and the latter as a force of direction.

One of the implications of merging these two approaches into the integrated model is that an interaction should exist between religious institutional strength and denominational composition. Moreover, the nature of this interaction effect is expected to be opposite for suicide and homicide. As Unnithan et al. (1994) explain:

> The concept of statistical interaction provides another way of understanding how the integrated model ties together the forces of production and direction and their respective impacts on suicide and homicide rates. It follows from equations 6.1 and 6.2 that the suicide rate of a population is the product of the SHR and the LVR. Similarly, the homicide rate is the product of the LVR and 1 minus the SHR, the proportion of the population that chooses homicide over suicide . . . . . . This way of looking at the integrated model leads to a number of nonobvious conclusion that suggest that studies of either suicide or homicide rates in isolation from one another may overlook important factors that can affect their results. For example, the integrated model predicts that the attribution of blame for bad events has a greater effect on both suicide and homicide rates in settings characterized by high levels of frustration than it does in less frustrating environments. Similarly, frustration should have a greater effect on suicide rates than on homicide rates under conditions in which persons are culturally predisposed to take responsibility for their own

> bad outcomes. Conversely, frustration should be more closely related to homicide than to suicide rates under structural and cultural conditions encouraging external attributions of blame. (P. 99-100)

Unnithan et al. hypothesize about interactive effects pertaining to frustration and external attributions. I apply a similar logic to the preventive effects of religious institutions; specifically, the preventive effect of strong religious institutions on homicide rates should be attenuated in areas with a relatively high proportion of conservative Protestant denominations characterized by a tendency for the externalization of blame. Within the framework of the stream analogy, reductions in the flow of the current of lethal violence brought about by community religiosity will not be as influential on homicide rates in populations predisposed by denominational forces that direct lethal violence towards others because the share of the flow that remains is more likely to be directed to homicide. The moderating directional effect thus tends to counteract the reducing flow effect; this interaction can be represented schematically as follows:

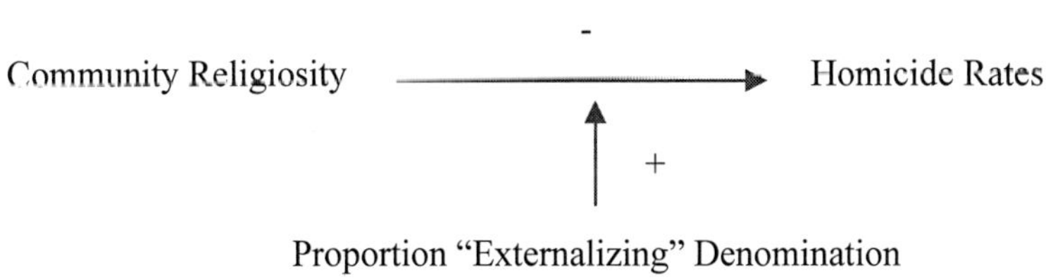

The hypothesized interaction for suicide rates is the reverse, applying an analogous logic. The preventive effect of strong religious institutions on suicide rates should be amplified in areas with a relatively high proportion of Protestant denominations characterized by a tendency for the externalization of blame. Again returning to the stream analogy, the "reduction in the flow" of pressures towards suicidal violence is reinforced when the size of the externalizing denomination is large because the lethal forces that manage to "fall over the dam" are likely to be directed towards homicide rather than suicide.

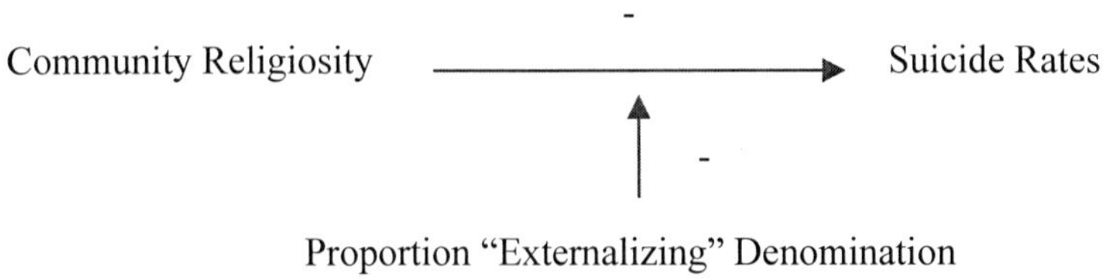

Support for the conditional effects model might help account for inconsistent findings concerning institutional effects of religion on suicide and homicide. Given the hypothesized interaction, the effects of community religiosity on both suicide and homicide will depend on the denominational composition of the specific communities included in the sample. It further follows that the effect of community religiosity on the suicide-homicide ratio will also be sample-specific, reflecting the combination of the effects on the respective components of this ratio.

Contextual Effects and the Ecological Fallacy

Finally, it is important to consider the dangers of committing the ecological fallacy when addressing macro-sociological processes. As Robinson (1950) first demonstrated, it is logically invalid to infer relationships at the micro-level from macro-level data. Consequently, it is not the intent of this research to make claims about relationships that might exist between individual religious participants and individual risk of lethal violence. Instead, consistent with research tradition on the contextual effects of religion, this research focuses exclusively on the macro-sociological connections between the risk of lethal violence for all members of the community and both levels of community religiosity and denominational composition of communities. The findings emanating from this research, therefore, will not reveal whether religious individuals are at lower risk of being involved in lethal violence or whether members of particular religious denominations are more likely to commit homicide over suicide. What is proposed, however, is that the level of religious institutional strength has an impact on the risk of lethal violence for the community as a whole, and that the presence of denominational groups that externalize blame can affect the likelihood that lethal violence within that community will manifest as homicides instead of suicides.

CHAPTER 4:

Data and Methods

The purpose of this chapter is to explain the data and methodological procedures necessary to analyze each of the three models proposed in the previous chapter. This chapter will begin with an explanation of the decision to focus on counties as a unit of analysis. A brief description of the two data sources used to collect data for the models will follow, including a discussion of the methodological limitations of lethal violence rates and religious affiliation data. Next, this chapter will provide a detailed listing of the independent, dependent and control variables in each model, including some descriptive statistics. Finally, this chapter will lay out the analytic strategy of the study by explaining the statistical procedures and hypotheses used to test each of the three models.

UNIT OF ANALYSIS

This study constitutes a cross-sectional analysis of lethal violence across U.S. counties centered on the year 2000. While the majority of past research on homicide and suicide has focused on cities, Metropolitan Statistical Areas, or featured state-level data (Land, McCall, and Cohen 1990; McCall, Land, and Parker 2010; Parker, McCall, and Land 1999; Stack 2000a; Stack 2000b; Wray, Colen, and Pescosolido 2011), there are several reasons for turning attention to counties as a unit of analysis. The first and most practical reason is that counties represent the smallest macro-sociological unit of analysis for which measures of both forms of lethal violence and religiosity are available. Consequently, the theoretical traditions from which the hypothesized effects of religion on homicide and suicide are drawn have relied heavily on county-level analysis (for examples, see:

Beyerlein and Hipp 2005; Lanier 2010; Lee 2006; Lee, Bankston, Hayes, and Thomas 2007; Lee and Bartkowski 2004a; Lee and Bartkowski 2004b; Shihadeh and Winters 2010; Wu 2003; Wu 2004). Second, counties are frequently the focus of research on moral communities since religious institutions often produce social pressure on their communities through county-level legal processes. For example, Frendreis and Tatalovich (2010) noted that despite the modern cultural acceptance of alcohol in America, many evangelical Protestant-dominated counties continue to utilize local legal and political processes to ban or limit alcohol sales. Similarly research reported by Ulmer, Bader and Gault (2008) demonstrated that high levels of Christian homogeneity within counties appeared to increase the likelihood that courts would utilize incarceration over other punitive options in criminal sentencing.

Counties, consequently, are useful units of analysis since they represent a community large enough to share institutional structures (e.g., legal, political and religious) but still small enough to also share cultural commonalities. A third reason for utilizing counties as an appropriate unit of analysis is identified by Kposowa and Breault (1993), who point out that highly urbanized units of analysis such as cities or MSAs provide insufficient regional, racial and economic diversity to avoid high levels of collinearity between common control variables such as percent African American, poverty, economic inequality, and southernness.

Ideally, this study would examine the entire constellation of U.S. counties, but both count suppression in lethal violence data and undercounts in religion data generate significant challenges to analyzing sparsely populated counties. Traditional approaches to both suicide and homicide at the county level have focused predominantly on counties with large annual population counts of 100,000 or more (for examples, see: Breault 1986; Wu 2003; Wu 2004). However, contemporary research on homicide by Lee (2006) and by Osgood and Chambers (2000), and on suicide by Cutlip, Bankston and Lee (2010) has demonstrated the value of incorporating rural counties with populations of fewer than 100,000 residents.

To capture the widest range of structural and cultural differences among counties, efforts were made to include as many counties as possible in the analysis. To identify a suitable sample, each of the 3,140 counties in the United States was ranked by population size; then, beginning with the most populous, each county was added to the sample until the most populous county with suppressed lethal violence rates was reached. Following this procedure, the 1,048 most populous counties with non-suppressed lethal violence data were identified. Exactly one-third of the 3,140 counties in the United States fall within this population requirement, including every county of 42,500 residents or greater. Due to the difficulties presented with rare events (i.e., suicide and homicide) in small populations, an issue discussed in some detail below, this sample selection was justified. The counties included in this study contain 87.4 percent of the U.S. population. Counties do represent clear political boundaries, however, it is acknowledged that they may not represent religious boundaries inasmuch, as religious attendance patterns may cut across county borders in some cases.

DATA SOURCES

Religious Congregations & Membership

Data for community religiosity and denominational composition are both available through the Religious Congregations and Membership Study (RCMS) (Jones et al. 2002) collected at the start of each decade since 1950 by the Association of Statisticians of American Religious Bodies. This study focuses on data from the year 2000, the most recent data compilation available. One hundred and forty-nine of 285 religious groups participated in the 2000 data collection, which gathered both congregational membership and number of congregations for each county. Given the complex and varied ways in which congregations define their 'membership' Jones et al. provided the following guidelines:

> In an effort to achieve comparability of data, however, two major categories were established:
> MEMBERS: all individuals with full membership status; and
> TOTAL ADHERENTS: all members, including full members, their children and the estimated number of other participants who are not considered members; for example, the "baptized," "those not confirmed," "those not eligible for communion," "those regularly attending services," and the like. (2002:xv)

According to Jones et al. (2002), the major methodological concern with their data is the possible underrepresentation of historically African American denominations due to limited record keeping by these groups at the national level. Jones et al. consequently warn that the RCMS data may undercount religious membership in counties with large African American populations.

Finke and Scheitle (2005) pointed to both the absence of many denominations and the variance of undercounts across geographic regions as two further concerns with the 2000 RCMS. In particular, they noted that the 149 religious bodies surveyed in the RCMS represent roughly 89% of all religious adherents identified in the Yearbook of American and Canadian Churches (which the RCMS uses as its sampling frame). Finke and Sheitle specifically noted that these undercounts are not evenly dispersed across counties and, as previously mentioned by Jones et al., are highly correlated with race. To reduce problems that may arise from these undercounts, Finke and Scheitle calculated count corrections based on their efforts to identify counts for all-black congregations absent from the RCMS data and based on ". . . calculated corrective multipliers to account for the percent of whites, blacks, or other groups who were missing from the RCMS" (p. 19). Although Finke and Scheitle's corrections do not resolve all the issues with undercounts in the RCMS, they do provide a more inclusive and accurate representation of religious participation than the original data and are consequently used in this study.

Two methodological issues arise from the use of the corrected rates. First, 12 of the 1,048 counties included in this study have adjusted religious adherence rates that exceed 100 percent of the population total. This anomaly is most likely caused by imprecision generated by Finke and Scheitle's state-level adjustments as they are applied to county-level data, or may be the result of religious institutions drawing congregants from neighboring counties. For the purpose of this research, each of those twelve counties were recoded as 100% adherence. Second, it should be noted that Finke and Scheitle did not develop an adjustment multiplier for Washington, D.C., since it is not part of any state. Consequently, for the purpose of this research, Washington, D.C. will be included using its non-adjusted adherence rate. However, given the sizable African American community in Washington, D.C, the models will also be run excluding the District of Columbia. In either case, the benefits of using the corrected data to improve accuracy in counties with large black populations outweigh the limited discrepancies present in the data.

Vital Statistics

Both homicide and suicide data will be collected from the Centers for Disease Control's (CDC) National Vital Statistics System (NVSS). The NVSS aggregates all birth, death, marriage and divorce certificates issued in the United States and its territories. Given the overall rarity of lethal violence events and the small populations of many counties, it has become *pro forma* in cross-sectional violence research to calculate multi-year homicide or suicide rates spanning a period of either three years (e.g., Faupel, Kowalski, and Starr 1987; Kposowa, Breault, and Harrison 1995; Lee 2006; Whitt 2006; Wu 2003) or four years (e.g., Kowalski and Duffield 1990; Rivera, Chu, and Loftin 2002; Rosenfeld, Messner, and Baumer 2001). Also, since NVSS fatality data for counties with nine or fewer lethal violence deaths are suppressed for privacy reasons, combining counts over multiple years becomes necessary to access data for many of the moderately populated counties. To limit the effect of lethal violence's rarity in less populous counties and over short periods of time, as well as to reduce data loss from suppressed counts, the total numbers of homicides, suicides and intentional deaths occurring from 1999 to 2002 for each county were gathered from the compressed mortality file on the CDC Wonder system. By using this procedure, suicide and lethal violence counts were available for all 1,048 counties included in the study, but homicide counts were suppressed for 318 counties. Since both the lethal violence and suicide counts were present for the counties in which homicide was suppressed, the suppressed homicide counts were calculated by subtracting the county suicide count from its lethal violence count. Homicide, suicide, and lethal violence rates were then calculated by dividing each county's count by the sum of the county's population for each of the same four years.

In addition to the limitations presented by suppressed counts, two other methodological concerns with regards to lethal violence data are worth noting. First, Pridemore (2005) warns of the limitations of analyzing homicide rates at the county level with regards to small population counties (e.g., under 100,000 residents), because small discrepancies (under- or over-reported population size, unreported homicides, or under-reported homicides) could radically impact the county's homicide rate. Pridemore expresses particular concern for studies that disaggregate homicide rates, since demographic data are available on an even smaller number of cases, and each demographic group equals an even smaller number of cases. This study lessens these concerns by combining multiple years of non-disaggregated homicide counts and excluding counties with single year populations below 42,500 residents, thus ensuring that each included county's homicide, suicide, and lethal violence totals are based on a minimum population base of 170,000 resident/years.

Second, Douglas (1967), in his book *The Social Meanings of Suicide*, critiqued official suicide statistics by noting the uncertainty introduced into data collection by the lack of consistent social agreement on labeling a death a suicide.

> The primary difficulty with such definitions is in determining whether or not the individual actually killed himself. The case of the individual who writes a suicide note and then shoots himself is a clear case, but many cases of suicide are in fact more or less equivocal or debatable. For example, in the case of an individual who "jumps or falls" from a high place or who is found dead of barbiturate poisoning the question is often raised whether the case was suicidal or accidental. The term "suicide," as a mode of death used by coroners in the certification of death, is a medico-legal term, and includes, as a *sine qua non*, the concept that the person played a major role in bringing about his own demise, and that his intention in his behavior was to die. It should be obvious that statistics on suicide can be greatly influenced (in any locale or for any temporal period) by the manner in which these equivocal deaths are labeled. For example, one major city of the United States had only a consistently low number of suicides each year because the coroner does not label a case as "suicide" unless a note is found with the body. (P.185)

Consequently, Douglas concluded that suicide rates were only of use in understanding the "organizations and social processes that produce official suicide rates" (230) and not very helpful in measuring or understanding real suicide rates.

In response to Douglas's concerns, Pescosolido and Mendelsohn (1986) proposed an empirical test of the claim that suicide data may be systematically biased. Examining 1970 suicide rates for county groups alongside measures of variances in the medical examiner system across municipalities, Pescosolido and Mendelsohn conclude that suicides are indeed underreported, but that the coefficients for common sociological theories of suicide appear sufficiently robust to overcome any problems:

> . . . misreporting has little effect on the relationship between suicide rates and indicators of concepts in sociological theories of suicide. Whether or not misreporting is taken into account, the coefficients of social causation factors have the same sign and the same approximate magnitude. (P. 94)

As medical examiners have been increasingly professionalized, stricter and more detailed guidelines for the determination of suicide (e.g., Rosenberg, Davidson, Smith, Berman, Buzbee, Gantner, Gay, More-Lewis, Mills, and Murray 1988) have emerged to reduce errors in classification. More recently, Timmermans conducted an ethnographic examination of the medical examiners' profession to see if ". . . increased professionalization of death investigation has rendered suicide determination less equivocal . . ." (2005:312). He concluded that, while the process is still imperfect, third parties such as family members of the deceased have little influence on medical examiners' decisions. Timmermans further points out that the classification of suicide is more problematic in cases where preexisting chronic medical conditions exist, but less problematic in more violent deaths. Moreover, in a recent analysis of the influence of personnel and policy changes in medical examiner's offices in New York City on county-level suicide rates throughout New York State, Whitt (2006) concluded that future studies can mitigate some of the bias by sampling large numbers of counties over multiple years. Moreover, since the majority of inconsistencies in lethal violence rates occurs in counties with smaller populations (see: Wiersema, Loftin, and McDowall 2000), the present study minimizes these methodological concerns by only using data from the most populated U.S. counties.

MEASURES

Dependent Variables

The models examined in this research focus on four different dependent variables derived from the NVSS. Given the highly skewed nature of county homicide rates (see table 4.1), externally directed lethal violence will be measured as the natural logarithm of homicides per 100,000 county residents during 1999 – 2002 (plus a constant of 1.0 to avoid zero values). This transformation is necessary to meet the assumptions of a normal distribution and is common practice in the homicide literature (for examples see: Land, McCall, and Cohen 1990; Weisheit and Wells 2005). Internally directed lethal violence will be measured as suicides per 100,000 county residents during 1999 - 2002. Following Unnithan et al. (1994), the total lethal violence rate (LVR) is calculated for each county by adding the homicide and suicide rate, and the suicide-homicide ratio (SHR) will be calculated by dividing each county's suicide rate by the sum of the suicide and homicide rates. It is worth noting, as Fernquist (2002) pointed out, that this formulation of the SHR technically calculates the proportion of lethal violence that manifests as suicide but is not a ratio of the suicides to homicides as the name implies. Unnithan et al. do, however, acknowledge the confusing nature of the label but provide no real justification for mislabeling the formula as the 'suicide-homicide ratio'.

Table 4.1. Descriptive Statistics for Dependent Variables

Variables	Range	Mean	Std. Deviation	Skewness
LVR	5.300 – 50.390	16.590	5.627	1.247
Suicide rate	3.880 – 29.030	11.701	3.601	.810
Homicide rate	.000 – 39.800	4.90	4.20	3.00
Homicide rate (+1 [log])	.000 – 3.710	1.587	.595	.231
SHP	.130 – 1.000	.729	.148	-.874

Following Fernquist's suggestion, this study uses the more accurate label 'suicide-homicide proportion' (SHP). Table 4.1 details the descriptive statistics for these four dependent variables and reveals that the mean lethal violence rate for the counties included in this study is 16.590 per 100,000 residents. It is worth noting that suicide is more than twice as common (mean = 11.7) as homicide (mean = 4.9) in the sampled counties, which is further reflected in the mean for the suicide-homicide proportion (.729) which translates to an average county in the study experiencing 72.9 percent of its lethal violence as suicides.

Independent Variables

Three separate measures of community religious institutional strength appear throughout the religious institutional effects literature. While most studies have focused on the percentage of the population affiliated with a religious institution, a few have focused on congregations per capita or religious homogeneity. The present analysis examines the roles of all three measures since they each represent slightly different aspects of religious institutional strength. The proportion of county residents belonging to a religious institution directly reflects the pervasiveness of the moral community as originally envisioned by Stark and Bainbridge (1996). Among the counties included in this analysis, the rate of affiliation with religious institutions ranges from 20.1 percent to 100 percent, with the average county having roughly half of its residents belonging to religious institutions (see table 4.2 below). Congregations per 100,000 residents provides a different perspective on the institutional strength of religion in counties by highlighting the ". . . degree of access local residents have to religious institutions" (Lee and Bartkowski 2004a:20). The counties in this study averaged 114.647 congregations per 100,000 residents, or roughly one congregation for every 1,000 residents. This is an entirely reasonable number when we consider that the average congregation in American consists of only 75 regular members (Chaves 2011).

Finally, the degree of religious homogeneity provides a clearer picture of the potential uniformity among religious structures present within a county. Numerous scholars have measured religious diversity with the Simpson index (also known as the Herfindahl index), which calculates the likelihood that any two individuals chosen at random from the county's religious population will share similar religious affiliations (Bruce 2011). "This index is defined for any unit as: $1 - \sum(x_i/X)^2$. Where x_i is the number in subgroup i and X is the total population" (Land, McCall, and Cohen 1990:239). In the above equation total diversity would equal 1, while total uniformity would equal 0. Given the theoretical focus on homogeneity instead of diversity, this study employs a reversed version of the Simpson/Herfindahl index $\sum(x_i/X)^2$ which results in total diversity equaling 0 and total uniformity equaling 1. Furthermore, the reversed Simpson/Herfindahl index is calculated using broad religious groupings (mainline Protestant, evangelical Protestant, Catholic, Mormon, Orthodox Christian, Jewish, and Islamic) instead of individual places of worship, a decision that is consistent with findings by Ellison, Burr and McCall (1997). Ellison et al. report that it is unnecessary to calculate the Simpson/Herfindahl index using individual church memberships. Table 4.2 shows a wide range of diversity among the counties included in this study with regards to religious homogeneity. Counties range from total diversity to nearly total conformity, with the average county scoring near the middle of the diversity index (mean = .432).

Following the theoretical arguments laid out in chapter 3, denominational effects will focus on conservative Protestant communities as groups that foster community-wide externalization of blame. For the purpose of this research, two classification systems are employed to identify conservative Protestant denominations. First, each model is tested using the percentage of conservative Protestants identified for each county in the RCMS, including all of the denominations listed in the *Appendix*. This subset of Protestant denominations was chosen based on a combination of historical analysis and General Social Survey data. Frendreis and Tatalovich (2011) recently validated the RCMS's classifications with the Chaves scale, an independent measure of biblical inerrancy.

Blanchard, Bartkowski, Matthews and Kerley (2008) identify three distinct subgroups (fundamentalists, evangelicals and Pentecostals) within the conservative Protestant tradition that influence life expectancy in different ways. In particular, they argue that fundamentalists and Pentecostals respond to secular society via isolation, which should in turn limit their ability to contribute the larger community's attempts at combating public health threats. They also argue that evangelical Protestants respond to secular society by engaging it directly, which results in greater participation by evangelicals in community outreach and consequently allows the community as a whole to benefit from the social networks generated by evangelicals.

Table 4.2. Descriptive Statistics for Independent Variables.

Variables	Range	Mean	Std. Deviation	Skewness
Institutional Measures				
Percent Religiously Affiliated	20.110 – 100.000	48.554	13.334	.440
Congregations per 100,000 residents	31.970 – 326.050	114.647	54.548	.973
Simpson/Herfindhal index (reversed)	.000 – 0.940	.432	.139	.496
	Denominational Measures			
Percent Conservative Protestant	.180 – 80.750	16.789	14.478	1.097
Percent Pentecostal	.000 – 12.150	2.042	1.596	1.719
Percent Evangelical	.000 – 24.960	2.791	3.086	2.789
Percent Fundamentalist	.000 – 73.650	11.956	13.758	1.268

Given the inconsistencies among prior studies in how conservative Protestant groups were divided to study their influence on homicide and suicide, it seems most practical to analyze each of the three subgroups independently to identify any variance among fundamentalist, evangelicals and Pentecostals. See the *Appendix* for a list of the congregations that make up each classification.

Control Variables

One justification for examining lethal violence as a whole instead of focusing on external and internal manifestations is the fact that both homicide and suicide scholars have identified many common correlates. Following the suggestion of anti-aesthetic scholars (see: Burkett and White 1974), it is particularly important to account for other institutional influences that may disguise religion's influence on lethal violence as a whole. Accordingly, key structural variables identified by past researchers on homicide and suicide are included in each model.

Within the criminological literature, several structural variables have been identified as robust and consistent predictors of homicide -- namely, population density, economic deprivation, divorce rate, unemployment rate, and regional location (the South in particular) have all been vetted as causes of higher homicide rates (Land, McCall, and Cohen 1990; McCall, Land, and Parker 2010; Pridemore 2002). In one of the few county-level studies of key structural variables influencing homicide, Kposowa, Breault and Harrison (1995) identified percent black, percent divorced, located in South, and percent of families in poverty as strong determinants of homicide, along with population density and education. Similarly, Tcherni identified three key structural forces behind county-level homicide rates: ". . . poverty index (poverty + low education), racial composition (percent black), and family structure variable (percent divorced/separated)" (2011:486). Stack's (2000a; 2000b) reviews of the suicide literature identified education, urbanization, divorce, income inequality, and unemployment as indicators of county-level suicide rates. Based on the preceding reviews, the following control variables will be included.

Population density. Scholars in general assert that high levels of population density increase the risk of a number of social ills, including lethal violence (Choldin 1978). More recently, both branches of the lethal violence literature have identified population density as a significant county-level predictor for lethal outcomes (Beyerlein and Hipp 2005; Kposowa and Breault 1993). This research will follow the same procedures by employing the natural logarithm of county population density as a control variable. Based on prior research it is expected that population density will act as a force of production leading to increases in both homicide and suicide rates.

Secular institutional participation. Following Burkett and White's (1974) suggestion that involvement in non-religious institutions should also reduce anti-social behavior (i.e., suicide and homicide), several dimensions of secular institutional participation will be included in this analysis. Perhaps the most consistently significant predictor of both homicide (McCall, Land, and Parker 2010; Tcherni 2011) and suicide (Stack 2000b) at virtually all levels of analysis is family disruption. The overwhelming majority of researchers have conceptualized family disruption through various measures of divorce, which has been robustly connected to higher rates of both suicide and homicide. For this research, the percentage of residents currently divorced is used as a measure of disengagement from the nuclear family as an institution. Similarly, the percent unemployed will be included as a measure of participation in economic institutions. Unemployment percentages were obtained from the Bureau of Labor Statistics for the 1999 – 2002 time periods and logged due to a highly skewed distribution among the raw rates. Finally, the percentage of county residents over 18 who voted in the 2000 presidential election will be included as a measure of participation in political institutions. In general, it is expected that each of these three institutional participation measures will act as forces of production. Consequently, both percent divorced and percent unemployed should be positively correlated with the lethal violence rate while voter turnout should be negatively correlated with the lethal violence rate.

Population Turnover. Rapid population changes have long been associated with antisocial behavior at the neighborhood level (Sampson, Raudenbush, and Earls 1997) and at the MSA-level (South

1987). The percentage of residents who lived in a different county in 1995 will be used as a measure of population turnover, which should act as a force of production. Consequently, counties with large percentages of new residents are expected to experience higher rates of lethal violence.

Age composition. Although age appears significant in both branches of the lethal violence literature, most of the scholarship on suicide suggests an increased risk of suicide as the male population ages (e.g., McKeown, Cuffe, and Schulz 2006), while the homicide literature suggests higher rates among younger male populations (Fox 2006; Fox and Piquero 2003). Consequently, a county's age composition should act as a force of direction since aging populations ought to experience higher suicide rates and lower homicide rates while younger populations should experience the opposite. Following Baller et al.'s (2001) research on county-level homicide rates, the present research will use each county's median age for males as the measure of that county's male population's age.

Concentrated disadvantage. Prior research has also identified percent black, percentage of female-headed households with children, and percent in poverty as strong predictors of homicide rates. However, given the high levels of collinearity among these three variables, scholars often combine them into a measure of concentrated disadvantage (Land, McCall, and Cohen 1990; Sampson, Morenoff, and Earls 1999; Sampson, Raudenbush, and Earls 1997). This research will include a similar index for concentrated disadvantage generated by principal components factor analysis of four measures: percent black, percent female-headed families, percent in poverty for the year 2000, and the Gini coefficient gathered from the U.S. Census. The Gini index is often employed as a measure of relative deprivation since it measures to what extent the actual distribution of income differs from a hypothetical distribution in which every member receives an equal share (Morse 2004). County-level research on the integrated model by Wu (2003) has already demonstrated the significant positive relationship between the Gini index and the lethal violence rate. While concentrated disadvantage indexes are common in homicide research, there are no comparable measures in the suicide literature.

Consequently, this index should have a positive relationship on the homicide rate and no hypothesized relationship with the suicide rate.

Region. Both homicide and suicide scholarship have focused on significant regional differences. In particular, the South is generally accepted as a region of increased homicidal violence and decreased rates of suicidal violence. In their original test of the integrated model, Unnithan et al., (1994) examine the South's role in lethal violence rates and conclude that southern culture exhibits a profound influence on the SHR. In early research on this connection between southernness and violence, Ellison (1991) identified birth in the South as the strongest predictor of support for defensive interpersonal violence. Consequently, the current study will include percent of county population born in the census South (i.e., Alabama, Arkansas, Delaware, Florida, Georgia, Kentucky, Louisiana, Maryland, Mississippi, North Carolina, Oklahoma, South Carolina, Tennessee, Texas, Virginia, Washington D.C., and West Virginia) as obtained from the 2000 U.S. Census.

Summary. See table 4.3 for details of the descriptive statistics for each of the control variables outlined above.

ANALYTIC STRATEGY

In order to test the three models proposed in chapter three, ordinary least squares (OLS) regression will be used. There have been recent methodological concerns with applying OLS regression to count-based homicide data (see: Osgood 2000; Pridemore 2005), therefore serious consideration was taken in choosing the most appropriate statistical procedures. Although both Osgood and Pridemore raise important issues with the skewed nature of homicide counts, their concerns are primarily focused on disaggregated homicide data (i.e., race, gender, or age specific rates) and on counts from small units of analysis (i.e., census tracts, neighborhoods, or sparsely populated counties). The present research avoids both of these pitfalls by focusing on non-disaggregated homicide rates, in the most populated third of U.S. counties, over a four-year period of time. An examination of basic descriptive statistics along with histograms for each of the dependent variables confirmed that both the LVR and the suicide rate were normally distributed across the selected counties. Although the

Table 4.3. Descriptive Statistics for Control Variables.

Variables	Range	Mean	Std. Deviation	Skewness
Population Density (ln)	.880 – 11.110	5.260	1.268	.576
Median age of males	23.400 – 52.900	34.613	3.519	.066
Percent unemployed (ln)	.720 – 3.000	1.505	.307	.517
Percent born in census south	1.500 – 97.200	37.801	36.709	.358
Population turnover	4.800 – 51.800	20.428	7.205	.780
Voter turnout	23.790 – 79.08	51.544	8.299	-.109
Percent Divorced	4.700 – 15.700	9.907	1.674	.039
Disadvantage index	-1.988 – 4.621	.000	1.000	1.126

homicide rate did appear skewed, taking its natural logarithm provided a normally distributed variable that meets the requirements of OLS regression (see table 1).

Model I focuses exclusively on the institutional effects of religion on lethal violence, and can be expressed in the following equations:

(1)

Lethal Violence Rate = a + b_1 (community religiosity) + b_2 (population density log) + b_3 (median age of males) + b_4 (Gini index) + b_5 (% unemployed log) + b_6 (% born in south) + b_7 (population turnover) + b_8 (voter turnout) + b_9 (% divorced) + b_{10} (concentrated disadvantage index) + e

(2)

Homicide Rate = a + b_1 (community religiosity) + b_2 (population density log) + b_3 (median age of males) + b_4 (Gini index) + b_5 (% unemployed log) + b_6 (% born in south) + b_7 (population turnover) + b_8 (voter turnout) + b_9 (% divorced) + b_{10} (concentrated disadvantage index) + e

(3)

Suicide Rate = a + b_1 (community religiosity) + b_2 (population density log) + b_3 (median age of males) + b_4 (Gini index) + b_5 (% unemployed log) + b_6 (% born in south) + b_7 (population turnover) + b_8 (voter turnout) + b_9 (% divorced) + b_{10} (concentrated disadvantage index) + e

(4)

Suicide/Homicide Proportion = a + b_1 (community religiosity) + b_2 (population density log) + b_3 (median age of males) + b_4 (Gini index) + b_5 (% unemployed log) + b_6 (% born in south) + b_7 (population turnover) + b_8 (voter turnout) + b_9 (% divorced) + b_{10} (concentrated disadvantage index) + e

Based on the literature reviewed in chapter 3, community religiosity (either in the form of percent religious, places of worship per capita, or religious homogeneity) should have a negative effect on the lethal violence rate as an aggregate, and in both of its disaggregated forms (i.e., b_1 should be negative in equations 1-3). Furthermore, model I predicts that there will be no significant relationship between community religiosity and the SHP (i.e., $b_1 = 0$)

Model II shifts the focus to the denominational effects of religion on lethal violence and can also be expressed in four formulas:

(5)
Lethal Violence Rate = a + b_1 (community religiosity) + b_2 (externalizing denominations) + b_3 (population density log) + b_4 (median age of males) + b_5 (Gini index) + b_6 (% unemployed log) + b_7 (% born in south) + b_8 (population turnover) + b_9 (voter turnout) + b_{10} (% divorced) + b_{11} (concentrated disadvantage index) + e

(6)
Homicide Rate = a + b_1 (community religiosity) + b_2 (externalizing denominations) + b_3 (population density log) + b_4 (median age of males) + b_5 (Gini index) + b_6 (% unemployed log) + b_7 (% born in south) + b_8 (population turnover) + b_9 (voter turnout) + b_{10} (% divorced) + b_{11} (concentrated disadvantage index) + e

(7)
Suicide Rate = a + b_1 (community religiosity) + b_2 (externalizing denominations) + b_3 (population density log) + b_4 (median age of males) + b_5 (Gini index) + b_6 (% unemployed log) + b_7 (% born in south) + b_8 (population turnover) + b_9 (voter turnout) + b_{10} (% divorced) + b_{11} (concentrated disadvantage index) + e

(8)
Suicide/Homicide Proportion = a + b_1 (community religiosity) + b_2 (externalizing denominations) + b_3 (population density log) + b_4 (median age of males) + b_5 (Gini index) + b_6 (% unemployed log) + b_7 (% born in south) + b_8 (population turnover) + b_9 (voter turnout) + b_{10} (% divorced) + b_{11} (concentrated disadvantage index) + e

In this model, it is expected that the volume of adherents to denominations that externalize blame (percent conservative Protestant and its three sub-groups, percent evangelicals, percent Pentecostal, and percent fundamentalist) should be unrelated to the LVR (i.e., $b_2 = 0$ in equation 5). However, the denominational effects model further predicts that the percentage of adherents belonging to denominations that externalize blame should be positively correlated with the homicide rate (i.e., b_2 should be positive in equation 6). Finally the presence of these denominations should be negatively correlated with the suicide rate and the SHP (i.e., b_2 should be negative in equation 7 and 8).

The third and final model examines the hypothesis that the preventive effect of community religiosity on homicide rates should be attenuated in areas with a relatively high proportion of denominations characterized by a tendency for the externalization of blame. Moreover, the preventive effect of community religiosity on suicide rates should be amplified in areas with high proportions of externalizing denominations. This would follow from model II which predicts that conservative protestant communities should experience higher proportions of their lethal violence as homicide, and from model I, which predicts that any net increase in religiosity should reduce the net lethal violence rate. Model III can be expressed formally as:

(9)

Lethal Violence Rate = a + b_1 (community religiosity) + b_2 (externalizing denominations) + b_3 ((community religiosity) * (externalizing denominations)) + b_4 (population density log) + b_5 (median age of males) + b_6 (Gini index) + b_7 (% unemployed log) + b_8 (% born in south) + b_9 (population turnover) + b_{10} (voter turnout) + b_{11} (% divorced) + b_{12} (concentrated disadvantage index) + e

(10)

Homicide Rate = a + b_1 (community religiosity) + b_2 (externalizing denominations) + b_3 ((community religiosity) * (externalizing denominations)) + b_4 (population density log) + b_5 (median age of males) + b_6 (Gini index) + b_7 (% unemployed log) + b_8 (% born in south) + b_9 (population turnover) + b_{10} (voter turnout) + b_{11} (% divorced) + b_{12} (concentrated disadvantage index) + e

(11)

Suicide Rate = a + b_1 (community religiosity) + b_2 (externalizing denominations) + b_3 ((community religiosity) * (externalizing denominations)) + b_4 (population density log) + b_5 (median age of males) + b_6 (Gini index) + b_7 (% unemployed log) + b_8 (% born in south) + b_9 (population turnover) + b_{10} (voter turnout) + b_{11} (% divorced) + b_{12} (concentrated disadvantage index) + e

(12)

Suicide/Homicide Proportion = a + b_1 (community religiosity) + b_2 (externalizing denominations) + b_3 ((community religiosity) * (externalizing denominations)) + b_4 (population density log) + b_5 (median age of males) + b_6 (Gini index) + b_7 (% unemployed log) + b_8 (% born in south) + b_9 (population turnover) + b_{10} (voter turnout) + b_{11} (% divorced) + b_{12} (concentrated disadvantage index) + e

Consequently, the third model predicts a positive relationship between the mean-centered product term and the homicide rate (i.e., b_3 should be positive in equation 10) and a negative relationship between the mean-centered product term and both the suicide rate and the SHP (i.e., b_3 should be negative in equations 11 - 12). Finally, model III predicts that there will be no significant relationship between the mean-centered product term and the LVR (i.e., $b_3 = 0$ in equation 9).

CHAPTER 5:

Results for the Institutional Effects Model

This chapter examines the results of model I which tests the institutional effects hypothesis. Briefly, this hypothesis predicts that various indicators of the strength of the institution of religion (i.e., percent religiously affiliated, congregations per 100,000 population, and religious homogeneity) will be negatively related to homicide rates, suicide rates, and overall lethal violence rates. Moreover, these religious indicators are not expected to affect the suicide-homicide proportion (SHP). To establish a baseline model and to confirm that the data are in line with prior findings on both suicide and homicide, the initial regression model includes the control variables only (see model 0 in tables 5.1 thru 5.4). Selected measures of the institutional strength of religion are then entered into the equation singly (models 1 thru 3) and jointly (model 4). Following the mainstream Durkheimian approach, the first and second sections of this chapter examine suicide and homicide rates independently. The third and fourth sections then introduce concepts from integrated theory by reporting similar analyses for lethal violence rates and the SHP, respectively. The fifth and final section of this chapter discusses the overall results, and elaborate on their implications for the institutional effects hypothesis.

SUICIDE RATES

Table 5.1 (below) presents the ordinary least squares (OLS) results for the regressions of suicide rates on the control measures and measures of religious institutional strength. In model 0, as expected, all of the control measures are statistically significant; percent divorced (β = .398), median age of males (β = .284), population turnover (β = .170), percent unemployed (β = .103), and percent born in the south (β = .058) each exhibit a positive influence on county suicide rates. Also as expected, voter turnout (β = -.077) is negatively related to the suicide rate. Surprisingly, population density (β = -.321) showed a negative effect on suicide which was nearly as strong as the positive influence of percent divorced, a result which appears contrary to some prior literature, referenced in chapter four, which identified crowding and urbanization as causes of higher suicide rates. Wu's (2003) research on counties with 100,000 residents or more, however, found similar results with regards to population size and lethal violence. Wu discovered that, at least in urban counties, increased population played a significant role in reducing suicide rates and increasing homicide rates. Similarly, Kowalski, Faupel and Starr (1987) found a negative relationship between population size and the suicide rate in both highly urban and highly rural counties. Finally, in his review of research on suicide in rural communities, Hirsch (2006) found conflicting findings on the effects of population density on suicide, but he also noted that some scholars have theorized that denser populations may provide a protective effect against suicide by discouraging firearm access, reducing the focus on individuality, increasing access to psychiatric and trauma care, and providing stronger social networks and welfare safety nets. Overall, the baseline results provided by model 0 are consistent with prior macro-level research on suicide, indicating that there appear to be no major concerns of bias within the sample under investigation.

Moving beyond the control variables, table 5.1 also displays results of the analyses of the impact of three different measures of the institutional strength of religion within counties. Model 1 introduces percentage of the county population that is religiously affiliated as the first measure of religious institutional strength and, contrary to the hypothesis, shows a significant positive relationship between the measure and suicide rates (β = .076). Model 2 replaces percent religiously affiliated with congregations per 100,000 residents as a measure of religious institutional strength. Also contrary to the hypothesized effect, congregational density exhibits a significant positive effect (β = .124) on suicide rates. Model 3 examines religious homogeneity, the third and final measure of religious institutional strength. As hypothesized, religious homogeneity has a significant negative influence (β = -.175) on county-level suicide rates.

Model 4 includes all three measures of religious institutional strength. Each is statistically significant, with percent religiously affiliated (β = .104) and congregations per 100,000 (β = .096) exerting a more modest positive influence on the suicide rate than religious homogeneity, which exerts a somewhat stronger negative (β = -.175) influence. In model 4, divorce (β = .406), population density (β = -.302), median age of males (β = .297), population turnover (β = .203), unemployment (β = .120), voter turnout (β = -.097), and percent born in the South (β = .092) remain significant. The positive relationships between suicide and congregations per 100,000 residents and percent religiously affiliated both run contrary to the hypothesized effects and prior literature, suggesting that further analysis is warranted. This analysis will be presented both at the end of this chapter and in chapter 6.

HOMICIDE RATES

The results shown in table 5.2 follow the same logic as the prior analysis, with the natural logarithm of homicide rates serving as the dependent variable. Model 0 shows the results of the OLS regression with only control variables entered. As expected, the disadvantage index (β = .462) has a positive relationship with homicide. Also as expected, percent born in the South (β = .212), population density (β = .189), percent divorced (β = .133), and percent unemployed (β = .093) each increase the county homicide rate, while voter turnout (β = -.148) reduces it. The baseline model for homicide rates is thus consistent with the prior literature.

The addition of percent religiously affiliated (model 1) has no impact on the overall model. As predicted, congregations per 100,000 residents (model 2) does have a significant (β = -.078) negative influence on homicide. Similarly, religious homogeneity has a significant (β = -.051) negative influence on homicide rates when entered as the only religion variable (see model 3). The inclusion of all three measure of religious institutional strength (model 4) confirms the roles of both congregations per 100,000 residents (β = -.087) and religious homogeneity (β = -.064) in reducing county-level homicide rates.

Table 5.1: OLS Coefficients: Suicide Rates on Control Variables and Measures of Institutional Strength of Religion.

Variable	0		1		2		3		4	
	B	β	B	β	B	β	B	β	B	β
Constant	-4.062		-6.057		-6.584		-1.207		-5.488	
	(1.515)		(1.660)		(1.634)		(1.583)		(1.756)	
Population	-.913		-.914		-.726		-.990		-.857	
Density (ln)	(.073)	-.321**	(.072)	-.322**	(.086)	-.256**	(.073)	-.348**	(.087)	-.302**
Median Age	.290		.301		.273		.301		.304	
of Males	(.029)	.284**	(.029)	.294**	(.029)	.267**	(.028)	.294**	(.029)	.297**
Percent Born	.006		.004		.001		.014		.009	
in South	(.003)	.058*	(.003)	.038	(.003)	.014	(.003)	.142**	(.003)	.092**
Population	.085		.104		.105		.063		.102	
Turnover	(.014)	.170**	(.015)	.208**	(.014)	.210**	(.014)	.126**	(.016)	.203**
Voter turnout	-.034		-.038		-.023		-.042		-.042	
	(.014)	-.077*	(.014)	-.088**	(.014)	-.053	(.014)	-.098**	(.014)	-.097**
Percent	.856		.894		.875		.813		.874	
Divorced	(.052)	.398**	(.053)	.416**	(.052)	.407**	(.052)	.378**	(.053)	.406**
Disadvantage	-.078		-.064		-.033		-.150		-.108	
Index	(.115)	-.022	(.115)	-.018	(.115)	-.009	(.115)	-.042	(.114)	-.030
Percent										
Unemployed	1.209		1.335		1.342		1.140		1.407	
(ln)	(.377)	.103**	(.378)	.114**	(.376)	.115**	(.372)	.097**	(.371)	.120**

Table 5.1: OLS Coefficients: Suicide Rates on Control Variables and Measures of Institutional Strength of Religion (continued)

Variable	**0**		**1**		**2**		**3**		**4**	
	B	**β**	**B**	**β**	**B**	**β**	**B**	**β**	**B**	**β**
Percent Religiously Affiliated			.020						.028	
			(.007)	.076**					(.007)	.104**
Congregations per 100,000 residents					.008				.006	
					(.002)	.124**			(.002)	.096**
Religious Homogeneity							-3.946		-4.556	
							(.722)	-.152**	(.738)	-.175**
Adjusted R^2	.476		.479		.483		.490		.503	

Note: Numbers in parentheses are standard errors.

* $p < .05$ for a 2-tailed test; ** $p < .01$ for a 2-tailed test

Table 5.2: OLS Coefficients: Homicide Rates (ln) on Control Variables and Measures of Institutional Strength of Religion.

Variable	0		1		2		3		4	
	B	β	B	β	B	β	B	β	B	β
Constant	.834		.801		1.096		.993		1.182	
	(.216)		(.237)		(.234)		(.228)		(.255)	
Population	.089		.089		.069		.084		.062	
Density (ln)	(.01)	.189**	(.010)	.189**	(.012)	.147**	(.011)	.180**	(.013)	.131**
Median Age of	-.001		-.001		.000		-.001		.002	
Males	(.004)	.008	(.004)	.007	(.004)	.002	(.004)	-.004	(.004)	.012
Percent born in	.003		.003		.004		.004		.004	
South	(.000)	.212**	(.000)	.210**	(.000)	.240**	(.000)	.241**	(.000)	.269**
Population	.001		.001		-.001		-.001		-.002	
Turnover	(.002)	.009	(.002)	.012	(.002)	-.016	(.002)	-.006	(.002)	-.021
Voter turnout	-.011		-.011		-.012		-.011		-.013	
	(.002)	-.148**	(.002)	-.149**	(.002)	-.164**	(.002)	-.155**	(.002)	-.179**
Percent Divorced	.047		.048		.045		.045		.045	
	(.007)	.133**	(.008)	.134**	(.007)	.127**	(.007)	.126**	(.008)	.126**
Disadvantage	.275		.275		.27		.271		.266	
Index	(.016)	.462**	(.016)	.463**	(.016)	.454**	(.017)	.455**	(.017)	.447**
Percent	.179		.181		.165		.175		.168	
Unemployed (ln)	(.054)	.093**	(.054)	.094**	(.054)	.085**	(.054)	.091**	(.054)	.087**

Table 5.2: OLS Coefficients: Homicide Rates (ln) on Control Variables and Measures of Institutional Strength of Religion (continued)

Variable	0		1		2		3		4	
	B	**β**	**B**	**β**	**B**	**β**	**B**	**β**	**B**	**β**
Percent Religious Affiliated			.000 (.001)	.008					.001 (.001)	.032
Congregations per 100,000 residents					-.001 (.000)	-.078**			-.001 (.000)	-.087**
Religious Homogeneity							-.220 (.104)	-.051*	-.273 (.107)	-.064*
Adjusted R^2	.610		.610		.613		.611		.615	

Note: Numbers in parentheses are standard errors.

* $p < .05$ for a 2-tailed test; ** $p < .01$ for a 2-tailed test

LETHAL VIOLENCE RATES

Table 5.3 (below) displays the analysis of the effects of religious institutional strength on the lethal violence rate. Looking at the influence of the eight control measures, model 0 shows positive correlations between the disadvantage index (β = .430), percent divorced (β = .315), median age of males (β = .158), population turnover (β = .113), percent unemployed (β = .115), and percent born in South (β = .122) and the overall lethal violence rate. Voter turnout (β = -.073) and population density (β =- .063) both have significant negative correlations with the lethal violence rate. Percent divorced, percent unemployed, and voter turnout, each of the three measures of secular institutional strength, are the only control measures to behave as predicted in both the lethal violence analysis and the disaggregated analyses. The positive and significant relationship between population turnover and the lethal violence rate does occur as predicted, but as with the findings for median age of males, percent born in the South, and the disadvantage index, the positive effect on lethal violence appears to be driven by a significant positive relationship with either homicide or suicide, but not both. It is difficult to interpret these findings without also taking into account the effects of these variables on the suicide-homicide proportion.

Introducing percent religiously affiliated into the regression (model 1) has no significant effect on the regression. Model 2 replaces percent religiously affiliated with congregations per 100,000 (β = .062), which has a significant positive effect on the lethal violence rate. In contrast, model 3 finds a negative relationship between religious homogeneity (β = -.149) and lethal violence. Finally, model 4 includes all three measures of religious institutional strength. The results reveal that percent religiously affiliated (β = .078) is positively correlated with lethal violence and religious homogeneity is (β = -.168) is negatively correlated with lethal violence. Including all three measures of religious institutional strength also reveals the lack of a significant relationship between congregations per 100,000 residents and the lethal violence rate.

Table 5.3: OLS Coefficients: Lethal Violence Rates on Control Variables and Measures of Institutional Strength of Religion.

Variable	**0**		**1**		**2**		**3**		**4**	
	B	**β**	**B**	**β**	**B**	**β**	**B**	**β**	**B**	**β**
Constant	-4.296 (2.343)		-6.106 (2.574)		-6.284 (2.542)		.073 (2.449)		-3.851 (2.74)	
Population Density (ln)	-.278 (.112)	-.063*	-.278 (.112)	-.063*	-0.13 (0.134)	-.029	-.395 (.113)	-.089**	-.317 (.135)	-.071*
Median Age of Males	.252 (.044)	.158**	.262 (.045)	.164**	0.239 (0.045)	.150**	.269 (.044)	.168**	.279 (.045)	.175**
Percent born in South	.019 (.004)	.122**	.017 (.004)	.110**	0.015 (0.005)	.100**	.031 (.005)	.204**	.027 (.005)	.179**
Population Turnover	.088 (.021)	.113**	.105 (.023)	.135**	0.104 (0.022)	.133**	.055 (.022)	.070*	.091 (.024)	.117**
Voter turnout	-.05 (.021)	-.073*	-.054 (.021)	-.079*	-0.041 (0.021)	-.061	-.063 (.021)	-.093**	-.067 (.022)	-.099**
Percent Divorced	1.059 (.08)	.315**	1.093 (.083)	.325**	1.074 (0.081)	.319**	.994 (.08)	.296**	1.056 (.082)	.314**
Disadvantage Index	2.419 (.178)	.430**	2.431 (.178)	.432**	2.454 (0.179)	.436**	2.308 (.177)	.410**	2.338 (.177)	.415**

Table 5.3: OLS Coefficients: Lethal Violence Rates on Control Variables and Measures of Institutional Strength of Religion (continued)

Variable	**0**		**1**		**2**		**3**		**4**	
	B	**β**	**B**	**β**	**B**	**β**	**B**	**β**	**B**	**β**
Percent Unemployed (ln)	2.109 (.583)	.115**	2.224 (.587)	.121**	2.214 (0.585)	.121**	2.003 (.576)	.109**	2.259 (.578)	.123**
Percent Religiously Affiliated			.019 (.011)	.044					.033 (.011)	.078**
Congregations per 100,000 residents					.006 (.003)	.062*			.004 (.003)	.040
Religious Homogeneity							-6.041 (1.118)	-.149**	-6.805 (1.152)	-.168**
Adjusted R^2	.486		.487		.488		.500		.504	

Note: Numbers in parentheses are standard errors.

* $p < .05$ for a 2-tailed test; ** $p < .01$ for a 2-tailed test

Table 5.4: OLS Coefficients: Suicide-Homicide Proportion on Control Variables and Measures of Institutional Strength of Religion.

Variable	0		1		2		3		4	
	B	**β**	**B**	**β**	**B**	**β**	**B**	**β**	**B**	**β**
Constant	.663 (.051)		.642 (.057)		.547 (.055)		.670 (.055)		.547 (.060)	
Population Density (ln)	-.035 (.002)	-.303**	-.035 (.002)	-.303**	-.027 (.003)	-.229**	-.035 (.003)	-.304**	-.027 (.003)	-.230**
Median Age of Males	.004 (.001)	.102**	.004 (.001)	.105**	.004 (.001)	.084**	.004 (.001)	.103**	.004 (.001)	.085**
Percent born in South	-.001 (.000)	-.137**	-.001 (.000)	-.142**	-.001 (.000)	-.186**	-.001 (.000)	-.131**	-.001 (.000)	-.184**
Population Turnover	.001 (.000)	.046*	.001 (.001)	.056*	.002 (.000)	.091**	.001 (.000)	.044	.002 (.001)	.092**
Voter turnout	.002 (.000)	.107**	.002 (.000)	.104**	.002 (.000)	.135**	.002 (.000)	.106**	.002 (.000)	.133**
Percent Divorced	.005 (.002)	.059**	.006 (.002)	.064**	.006 (.002)	.069**	.005 (.002)	.058**	.006 (.002)	.069**
Disadvantage Index	-.074 (.004)	-.504**	-.074 (.004)	-.503**	-.072 (.004)	-.490**	-.075 (.004)	-.505**	-.072 (.004)	-.491**

Table 5.4: OLS Coefficients: Suicide-Homicide Proportion on Control Variables and Measures of Institutional Strength of Religion (continued)

Variable	0		1		2		3		4	
	B	β	B	β	B	β	B	β	B	β
Percent Unemployed (ln)	-.030 (.013)	-.063*	-.029 (.013)	-.061*	-.024 (.013)	-.051	-.031 (.013)	-.064*	-.024 (.013)	-.050
Percent Religious Affiliated			.000 (.000)	.019					.00005 (.000)	.004
Congregations per 100,000 residents					.000 (.000)	.139**			.000 (.000)	.138**
Religious Homogeneity							-.010 (.025)	-.010	-.005 (.025)	-.005
Adjusted R^2	.639		.639		.649		.639		.648	

Note: Numbers in parentheses are standard errors.

* $p < .05$ for a 2-tailed test; ** $p < .01$ for a 2-tailed test

SUICIDE-HOMICIDE PROPORTION

The results of the analysis of the impact of the control variables on the SHP, reported in table 5.4 (above), logically follow from the effects reported in the disaggregated analyses (tables 5.1 and 5.2), which reflect the respective effects on suicide rates and homicides rates, the components of the proportion. In particular, voter turnout (β = .107), median age of males (β = .106), percent divorced (β = .059), and population turnover (β = .046) are all positively correlated with the SHP, meaning that increases in these measures should result in a greater proportion of lethal events manifesting as suicides than homicides within a county. Conversely, the disadvantage index (β = -.504), population density (β = -.303), percent born in South (β = -.137), and percent unemployed (β = -.063) each exhibit a negative relationship with the SHP; thus, as these four measures increase, lethal violence will be more likely to manifest as homicides than suicides.

The addition of either percent religiously affiliated (model 1) or religious homogeneity (model 3) has no impact on the SHP regression, as neither of these measures is statistically significant. However, congregations per 100,000 residents (β = .139) is positively correlated with the SHP, suggesting that an increase in congregations within a county would shift more lethal violence toward suicides. This effect remains statistically significant when all three measures of religious institutional strength are included in the analysis (model 4). The finding of a positive effect of congregation numbers is contrary to the hypothesis of no relationship between religious indicators and the direction of lethal violence one way or another. However, the effect of congregations on the SHP could be anticipated from the separate analyses of homicide and suicide. The variable has a positive effect on suicide rates and a negative effect on homicide rates, leading one to anticipate that the association of congregations per 100,000 with SHP would be positive. A final noteworthy finding is that percent unemployed is no longer significantly related with the SHP when all religion variables are included. Since percent unemployed demonstrates a significant positive relationship with both suicide and homicide as well as lethal violence, it is most likely operating as a force of production for lethal violence. Similarly, the significant negative relationship between religious homogeneity and homicide, suicide, and lethal violence along with the lack of a statistically significant relationship with the SHP also supports the hypothesis that religious homogeneity inhibits the production of lethal violence.

FURTHER ANALYSIS

Prior research has developed three different approaches to conceptualizing the institutional strength of religion (percent religiously affiliated, congregations per 100,000 residents, and religious homogeneity). Research on the institutional effects of religion has thus far been limited to analyses of the major forms of lethal violence separately (i.e., suicide or homicide). In contrast, findings presented earlier pertain to relationships between the different measures of religious institutional strength and suicide rates, homicide rates, lethal violence rates, and the SHP.

Examining county-level suicide rates alone, it appears that counties with high percentages of religiously affiliated residents and high density of religious congregations are at the greater risk for high rates of suicide, while religiously homogenous counties are lower risk. On the other hand, switching the focus to homicide rates shows no effect of percent religiously affiliated but a deterrent effect for counties with high levels of congregational density and religious homogeneity. Employing the integrated model reveals a positive relationship between percent religiously affiliated and the lethal violence rate; this appears to be driven solely by the influence of percent religiously affiliated on suicide since no significant relationship exists between percent religiously affiliated and homicide. Using the integrated model approach, congregation density appears to have no net impact on the lethal violence rate and a positive effect on the SHP. Religious homogeneity, however, plays a significant role in reducing county lethal violence rates, but has no effect on the SHP.

Based on the above analyses, we can see that percent religiously affiliated is associated with higher suicide and total lethal violence rates despite theoretical expectations to the contrary. One possible explanation for this higher level of internalized lethal violence in counties with large numbers of religious members is that higher suicide rates could be due to more suicides among non-religiously affiliated populations (Day 1987), as those individuals experience higher rates of isolation and alienation from communities that normalize formal institutional religious participation. While this concept is impossible to test directly without data on individual religious affiliation of suicide victims, it should be possible, using available data, to identify whether or not communities with large numbers of bridging social capital religious groups (such as mainline Protestants) are less likely to experience higher suicide rates than are counties with large number of bonding social capital religious groups (such as conservative Protestants). This hypothesis will be further examined in chapter 6.

Interaction Term

Another possible explanation for the association between percent religiously affiliated and higher suicide and lethal violence rates is that an interaction may exist between percent religiously affiliated and the level of homogeneity within a county. Specifically, counties with large percentages of religious members and low levels of religious homogeneity may experience more suicide due to the fractured nature of religious institutions or communities of that county. In contrast, counties with high percentages of religious members and high levels of religious homogeneity may be expected to experience lower suicide rates as their religious institutions gain strength from religious uniformity and ubiquity. Model 5 in table 5.5 examines this hypothesis by adding an interaction term for percent religiously affiliated and religious homogeneity into the suicide model. The interaction term is statistically significant (β = .080), but interestingly in the opposite direction than predicted. Specifically, it was hypothesized that the impact of percent religiously affiliated on the suicide rate would be positive in religiously diverse counties and negative in religiously homogeneous counties. However, it appears that for counties with an average amount of religious homogeneity, each percent increase in religious membership increases the suicide rate by .029. The positive sign of the product term implies that this increasing effect of religious membership on suicide rates becomes even stronger as religious homogeneity increases. The results also indicate that in counties with an average level of religiously affiliated residents, each unit increase in religious homogeneity results in a 5.516 decline in the suicide rate. This protective effect of religious homogeneity lessens as religious membership grows. A graphical representation of this interaction can be seen in Figure 5.1, which depicts the expected values of the suicide rate when the percent religiously affiliated is at 20, 60, and 100, when the Simpson/Herfindahl index is either one standard deviation above or one standard deviation below the mean. As the graph shows, when religious homogeneity is high, increases in the percent religiously affiliated are expected to increase the suicide rate slightly more than when religious homogeneity is low.

Table 5.5: OLS Coefficients: suicide rates on the mean centered product term (Percent Religious x Religious Homogeneity).

Variable	4		5	
	B	β	B	β
Constant	-5.488 (1.756)		-5.761 (1.628)	
Population Density (ln)	-.857 (.087)	-.302**	-.832 (.087)	-.293**
Median Age of Males	.304 (.029)	.297**	.303 (.029)	.296**
Percent Born in South	.009 (.003)	.092**	.009 (.003)	.094**
Population Turnover	.102 (.016)	.203**	.101 (.015)	.203**
Voter turnout	-.042 (.014)	-.097**	-.046 (.014)	-.106**
Percent Divorced	.874 (.053)	.406**	.850 (.053)	.395**
Disadvantage Index	-.108 (.114)	-.030	-.130 (.113)	-.036
Percent Unemployed (ln)	1.407 (.371)	.120**	1.277 (.371)	.109**
Percent Religiously Affiliated	.028 (.007)	.104**	.029 (.007)	.108**
Congregations per 100,000 residents	.006 (.002)	.096**	.008 (.002)	.117**
Religious Homogeneity	-4.556 (.738)	-.175**	-5.516 (.794)	-.212**
Percent religious x religious homogeneity			.123 (.038)	.080**
Adjusted R^2	.503		.507	

Note: Numbers in parentheses are standard errors.
* p < .05 for a 2-tailed test; ** p < .01 for a 2-tailed test

Figure 5.1: Graph of Interaction Between Religiously Affiliated and Religious Homogenity

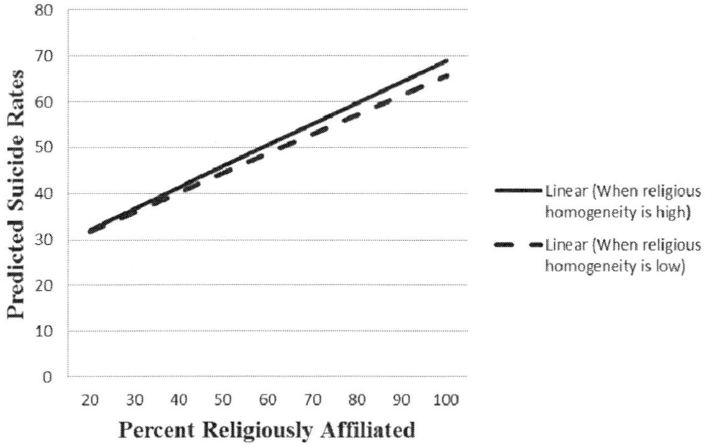

The finding that congregations per 100,000 residents acts as a force of direction, directing lethal violence toward suicides and away from homicides, and not as a force of production seems similarly confounding. This influence of congregations per 100,000 residents on the SHP, however, is not without precedent. Prior research by Beyerlein and Hipp (2005) identified negative relationships between the homicide rate and evangelical congregations per 100,000 residents, mainline congregations per 100,000, and Catholic congregations per 100,000. In contrast, Walker's (2009) analysis of suicide rates found positive relationships with mainline congregations per 100,000 and Catholic congregations per 100,000. Thus far, no theoretical explanation has been advanced in the literature to account for the positive effect of numbers of congregations on suicide rates, however, there are several possible explanations for these findings.

First, the processes that underlie the effect of congregations per capita on homicide may be fundamentally different than those for suicide, and thus the integrated model would be inappropriate for explaining these conditions. Second, the assumption that congregations per capita adequately measures institutional strength of religious communities could be incorrect. Third, congregational effects may be denomination-dependent (e.g. Beyerlein and Hipp 2005; Walker 2009), in which case it could be useful to assess the impacts of specific denominations of congregations per capita on model I. This particular hypothesis will be tested in chapter 6.

Religious homogeneity did, however, perform as predicted by reducing rates of suicide, homicide, and lethal violence. The majority of the prior literature has relied on either participation rates or number of congregations as the central focus for measuring religious institutional strength, so it is surprising to find that homogeneity, which has been utilized in only one prior study on suicide (Ellision, Burr, and McCall 1997), appears to be the measure that is in accord with these empirical results. Although moral community scholars have historically measured the strength of a community's religious institutions using levels of religious participation (see: Regnerus 2003; Stark 1996; Stark and Bainbridge 1996; Stark, Kent, and Doyle 1982), it now seems warranted to devote greater attention to the uniformity of a religious community's message (homogeneity) than has been the case in the past. As Ellision et al. (1997) suggested in their research on suicide, it appears that moral communities form more easily, operate more effectively, and endure longer when they are relatively homogenous. The present findings further confirm the robust nature of the relationship between religious homogeneity and violence, first by replicating Ellison et al.'s findings and then by extending their research beyond suicide, identifying a similar relationship between religious homogeneity and homicide. With this line of argument in mind, the institutional effects model for religion's influence on lethal violence at the county level seems correct if religious institutional effects are conceptualized as religious homogeneity.

Net Regression

Given the different metrics by which suicide (i.e., rates per 100,000) and homicide (i.e., rates per 100,000 logged) are measured for this study, it is difficult to make informal comparisons between the effects of each independent variable on the two forms of lethal violence. The integrated model works around this problem by combining homicide and suicide rates into a single measure of lethal violence. However, the above results provide little evidence of the control measures or the measures of religious institutional strength influencing both suicide and homicide in the same way. To test whether or not the independent variables have significantly different effects on both dependent variables, Cohen, Brook, Cohen, Velez and Garcia (1990) developed a procedure they term 'net regression'. In essence, net regression is a test of the relationship of risk factors to different outcome variables regardless of the metric in which those outcomes are measured. They describe the procedure as follows:

> ... an ordinary least-squares equation is produced for each of two standardized dependent variables, Y and Z, using all risk factors of interest....The two predicted or estimated dependent variables, Y̌ and Ž, are then produced. Their equations are, of course, the sum of the regression-weighted risk factors plus a constant. This sum for Y̌ is then subtracted from Z, and this new variable, Z- Y̌, is regressed on the original set of predictors (risk factors). The overall R for this equation and its associated F provides a test of the significance of the aggregate differences in risk factors, and each partial regression coefficient and its t indicates the magnitude and significance of the difference in risk for each variable (Cohen et al. 1990:249).

By employing this net regression procedure, it should be possible to determine if median age of males, population turnover, and percent religious affiliated are each significantly correlated with suicide rates but not homicide rates (as Tables 5.1 and 5.2 indicate), or whether these variables are significantly related to homicide and suicide (as suggested by Table 5.3) but play a significantly larger role in suicide rates.

The results of the net regression (see Table 5.6) reveal that the differences in the strength of each independent variable's correlation with suicide rates and homicide rates are significant for all but one measure (unemployment). Among the control variables, population density, percent southern-born, and the disadvantage index were each more strongly related to homicide rates than suicide rates. Median age of males, residential stability, voter turnout, and percent divorced were each more strongly related to suicide rates. For the three measures of religious institutional strength, both percent religiously affiliated and congregations per 100,000 were more highly related to suicide rates, while religious homogeneity was more highly related to homicide rates.

Table 5.6: Net Regression Analysis: Significant Differences in Risk Factors

Variable	Suicide	Homicide	Suicide-Homicide
Population Density (ln)	-.302**	.131**	-.341**
Median Age of Males	.297**	.012	.081**
Percent Born in South	.092**	.269**	-.005**
Population Turnover	.203**	-.021	.031**
Voter turnout	-.097**	-.179**	.010**
Percent Divorced	.406**	.126**	.168**
Disadvantage Index	-.030	.447**	-.477**
Percent Unemployed (ln)	.120**	.087**	.108
Percent Religiously Affiliated	.104**	.032	.005**
Congregations per 100,000 residents	.096**	-.087**	.003**
Religious Homogeneity	-.175**	-.064*	-.806**

* $p < .05$ for a 2-tailed test; ** $p < .01$ for a 2-tailed test

In the final analysis, then, only three of the predictors included in model I operated as predicted by the hypothesis. As discussed early in this chapter, population density acts as a force of direction that reduces suicide and simultaneously increases homicide, in a manner that has no net effect on the lethal violence rate but a strong negative effect on the SHP. Unemployment, on the other hand, acts as a force of production, increasing the flow of lethal violence by increasing both the suicide and the homicide rates while exerting no influence on the SHP. Finally, the level of religious homogeneity within a county plays a significant role in reducing the flow of lethal violence, as both suicide and homicide rates were lower in counties with high rates of religious homogeneity. These conclusions must be regarded for now as somewhat tentative, given that denominational effects have not been considered. These effects are the focus of the next chapter.

CHAPTER 6:

Results for the Denominational Effects Model

This chapter begins with an examination of the results of model II, which tests the denominational effects hypothesis. To review briefly, this hypothesis predicts that the prevalence of conservative Protestant religious affiliation will have a negative effect on county suicide rates, a positive effect on homicide rates, no effect on the lethal violence rates, and a negative effect on the SHP. The first section examines the results of OLS regressions of suicide rates on selected religious denominations identified for their theorized propensity to externalize blame. The second, third and fourth sections address similar analyses on homicide rates, lethal violence rates and the SHP, respectively. The analysis then turns to an assessment of model III, which predicts an interaction between religious homogeneity and conservative Protestant religious affiliation. Specifically, this final hypothesis predicts that the interaction term should be positively correlated with suicide, but negatively correlated with homicide. The fifth and final section of this chapter will discuss the overall results, and identify their principal implications for the denominational effects hypothesis.

SUICIDE RATES

Table 6.1 (below) shows the OLS regression of suicide rates on measures of religious denominational differences. The first column of data reproduces model 4 from Table 4. Contrary to the hypothesized effects, neither evangelicals nor fundamentalists show any significant effect on suicide rates. Moreover, the positive significant correlation between percent Pentecostal and the suicide rate also runs counter to the hypothesized effects. This finding does, however, support Blanchard et al.'s (2008) assertion that conservative Christians should not be viewed as a single block when addressing public health issues, and partially supports their prediction that Pentecostals and fundamentalists may fare worse in preventing public health crises due to their closed-off attitude toward secular society. The inclusion of all three branches of conservative Protestants (models 8) does result in the loss of significance for percent born in the South but, given the prevalence of these groups across the Deep South, it is reasonable to believe that some collinearity may exist between these measures. In fact, the variance inflation factor (VIF) score for fundamentalist Protestants is 4.918 in model 8.

HOMICIDE RATES

Table 6.2 (below) shows the results for including the percentage of the county population that is conservative Protestant in the models predicting homicide rates. While percent evangelical has no statistically significant impact on the homicide rate, the percent fundamentalist ($\beta = .206$ in model 6) and percent Pentecostal ($\beta = .048$ in model 7) both have a significant positive correlation with homicide. The inclusion of all three subcategories of conservative Protestantism reveals that only percent fundamentalist ($\beta = .198$) remains statistically significant. It is noteworthy that, the impact of percent divorced on homicide rates is reduced by half when the fundamentalist measure is included in the model; additionally, a significant negative relationship between population turnover and homicide is revealed. Moreover, the mitigating effects of congregations per 100,000 and religious homogeneity on homicide are both nearly doubled by the inclusion of the fundamentalist measure.

LETHAL VIOLENCE RATES

As hypothesized in chapter 4, there is no significant relationship between the percent evangelical Protestant or the percent Pentecostal on the lethal violence rate (Table 6.3 below). However, a significant positive relationship exists between percent fundamentalist Protestant ($\beta = .096$) and the lethal violence rate, which would logically follow from the findings in tables 6.1 and 6.2. That relationship, however, disappears in model 8 when each of the three subgroups is included.

Table 6.1: OLS Coefficients: Suicide Rates on Control Variables and Measures of Religious Denominational Differences.

Variable	4		5		6		7		8	
	B	**β**	**B**	**β**	**B**	**β**	**B**	**β**	**B**	**β**
Constant	-5.488		-5.488		-5.144		-5.305		-5.129	
	(1.756)		(1.757)		(1.873)		(1.754)		(1.871)	
Population Density (ln)	-.857		-.857		-.864		-.858		-.861	
	(.087)	-.302**	(.087)	-.302**	(.088)	-.304**	(.087)	-.302**	(.088)	-.303**
Median Age of Males	.304		.304		.306		.308		.308	
	(.029)	.297**	(.029)	.297**	(.029)	.299**	(.029)	.301**	(.029)	.301**
Percent Born in South	.009		.009		.008		.008		.007	
	(.003)	.092**	(.003)	.092**	(.004)	.080*	(.003)	.080*	(.004)	.073
Population Turnover	.102		.102		.099		.099		.097	
	(.016)	.203**	(.016)	.203**	(.016)	.198**	(.016)	.198**	(.016)	.195**
Voter turnout	-.042		-.042		-.042		-.040		-.040	
	(.014)	-.097**	(.014)	-.097**	(.014)	-.096**	(.014)	-.092**	(.014)	-.092**
Percent Divorced	.874		.874		.860		.840		.834	
	(.053)	.406**	(.053)	.406**	(.059)	.400**	(.054)	.390**	(.060)	.388**
Disadvantage Index	-.108		-.108		-.106		-.098		-.097	
	(.114)	-.030	(.114)	-.030	(.114)	-.029	(.113)	-.027	(.114)	-.027
Percent Unemployed (ln)	1.407		1.407		1.390		1.317		1.309	
	(.371)	.120**	(.371)	.120**	(.372)	.119**	(.372)	.112**	(.373)	.112**

Table 6.1: OLS Coefficients: Suicide Rates on Control Variables and Measures of Religious Denominational Differences (continued)

Variable	4		5		6		7		8	
	B	β	B	β	B	β	B	β	B	β
Percent Religiously	.028		.028		.027		.028		.027	
Affiliated	(.007)	.104**	(.007)	.104**	(.008)	.099**	(.007)	.102**	(.008)	.100**
Congregations per 100,000	.006		.006		.006		.006		.006	
residents	(.002)	.096**	(.002)	.096**	(.002)	.088*	(.002)	.087**	(.002)	.084*
Religious Homogeneity	-4.556		-4.553		-4.712		-4.546		-4.633	
	(.738)	-.175**	(.744)	-.175**	(.796)	-.181**	(.737)	-.175**	(.800)	-.178**
Evangelical			.001						-.002	
			(.028)	.001					(.028)	-.001
Fundamentalist					.007				.003	
					(.013)	.025			(.013)	.013
Pentecostal							.130		.128	
							(.056)	.058*	(.057)	.057*
Adjusted R^2	.503		.503		.503		.505		.504	

Note: Numbers in parentheses are standard errors. * $p < .05$ for a 2-tailed test; ** $p < .01$ for a 2-tailed test

Table 6.2: OLS Coefficients: Homicide Rates (ln) on Control Variables and Measures of Religious Denominational Differences.

Variable	4		5		6		7		8	
	B	β	B	β	B	β	B	β	B	β
Constant	1.182		1.182		1.644		1.207		1.645	
	(.255)		(.256)		(.269)		(.255)		(.269)	
Population Density (ln)	.062		.061		.053		.061		.053	
	(.013)	.131**	(.013)	.131**	(.013)	.113**	(.013)	.131**	(.013)	.113**
Median Age of Males	.002		.002		.005		.003		.005	
	(.004)	.012	(.004)	.011	(.004)	.029	(.004)	.015	(.004)	.029
Percent born in South	.004		.004		.003		.004		.003	
	(.000)	.269**	(.000)	.268**	(.001)	.171**	(.000)	.259**	(.001)	.165**
Population Turnover	-.002		-.002		-.006		-.002		-.006	
	(.002)	-.021	(.002)	-.021	(.002)	-.067*	(.002)	-.026	(.002)	-.069*
Voter turnout	-.013		-.013		-.013		-.013		-.012	
	(.002)	-.179**	(.002)	-.177**	(.002)	-.178**	(.002)	-.175**	(.002)	-.173**
Percent Divorced	.045		.045		.026		.040		.024	
	(.008)	.126**	(.008)	.127**	(.008)	.074**	(.008)	.113**	(.009)	.067**
Disadvantage Index	.266		.265		.269		.267		.269	
	(.017)	.447**	(.017)	.446**	(.016)	.452**	(.017)	.449**	(.016)	.453**
Percent Unemployed (ln)	.168		.168		.145		.156		.136	
	(.054)	.087**	(.054)	.087**	(.054)	.075**	(.054)	.080**	(.054)	.070*

Table 6.2: OLS Coefficients: Homicide Rates (ln) on Control Variables and Measures of Religious Denominational Differences (continued)

Variable	4		5		6		7		8	
	B	β	B	β	B	β	B	β	B	β
Percent Religiously Affiliated	.001		.002		.000		.001		.000	
	(.001)	.032	(.001)	.034	(.001)	-.011	(.001)	.031	(.001)	-.009
Congregations per 100,000	-.001		-.001		-.002		-.001		-.002	
residents	(.000)	-.087**	(.000)	-.085**	(.000)	-.151**	(.000)	-.094**	(.000)	-.153**
Religious Homogeneity	-.273		-.279		-.483		-.272		-.480	
	(.107)	-.064*	(.108)	-.065**	(.114)	-.113**	(.107)	-.063*	(.115)	-.112**
Evangelical			-.002						-.002	
			(.004)	-.009					(.004)	-.010
Fundamentalist					.009				.009	
					(.002)	.206**			(.002)	.198**
Pentecostal							.018		.014	
							(.008)	.048*	(.008)	.037
Adjusted R^2	.615		.614		.623		.616		.624	

Note: Numbers in parentheses are standard errors. * $p < .05$ for a 2-tailed test; ** $p < .01$ for a 2-tailed test

Table 6.3: OLS Coefficients: Lethal Violence Rates on Control Variables and Measures of Religious Denominational Differences.

Variable	4		5		6		7		8	
	B	β	B	β	B	β	B	β	B	β
Constant	-3.851		-3.850		-1.822		-3.640		-1.802	
	(2.74)		(2.741)		(2.918)		(2.741)		(2.917)	
Population Density (ln)	-.317		-.313		-.355		-.318		-.349	
	(.135)	-.071*	(.135)	-.071*	(.137)	-.080**	(.135)	-.072*	(.137)	-.079*
Median Age of Males	.279		.284		.292		.283		.298	
	(.045)	.175**	(.045)	.177**	(.045)	.182**	(.045)	.177**	(.046)	.186**
Percent born in South	.027		.028		.020		.026		.020	
	(.005)	.179**	(.005)	.181**	(.006)	.133**	(.005)	.169**	(.006)	.131**
Population Turnover	.091		.091		.075		.088		.073	
	(.024)	.117**	(.024)	.116**	(.026)	.096**	(.024)	.112**	(.026)	.093**
Voter turnout	-.067		-.070		-.067		-.064		-.067	
	(.022)	-.099**	(.022)	-.103**	(.022)	-.098**	(.022)	-.095**	(.022)	-.099**
Percent Divorced	1.056		1.049		.975		1.017		.941	
	(.082)	.314**	(.082)	.312**	(.091)	.290**	(.085)	.302**	(.093)	.280**
Disadvantage Index	2.338		2.349		2.352		2.35		2.371	
	(.177)	.415**	(.178)	.417**	(.177)	.418**	(.177)	.418**	(.178)	.421**

Table 6.3: OLS Coefficients: Lethal Violence Rates on Control Variables and Measures of Religious Denominational Differences (continued)

Variable	4		5		6		7		8	
	B	β	B	β	B	β	B	β	B	β
Percent Unemployed (ln)	2.259		2.268		2.159		2.155		2.086	
	(.578)	.123**	(.578)	.124**	(.580)	.118**	(.581)	.118**	(.582)	.114**
Percent Religiously Affiliated	.033		.031		.024		.032		.023	
	(.011)	.078**	(.011)	.074**	(.012)	.057*	(.011)	.076**	(.012)	.054*
Congregations per 100,000	.004		.004		.001		.003		.000	
residents	(.003)	.040	(.003)	.036	(.004)	.010	(.003)	.033	(.004)	.003
Religious Homogeneity	-6.805		-6.69		-7.727		-6.794		-7.535	
	(1.152)	-.168**	(1.160)	-.165**	(1.240)	-.190**	(1.151)	-.167**	(1.247)	-.186**
Evangelical			.038						.035	
			(.044)	.021					(.044)	.019
Fundamentalist					.039				.036	
					(.020)	.096*			(.020)	.088
Pentecostal							.150		.129	
							(.088)	.043	(.088)	.037
Adjusted R^2	.504		.504		.506		.505		.506	

Note: Numbers in parentheses are standard errors. * $p < .05$ for a 2-tailed test; ** $p < .01$ for a 2-tailed test

Table 6.4: OLS Coefficients: Suicide-Homicide Proportion on Control Variables and Measures of Religious Denominational Differences.

Variable	4		5		6		7		8	
	B	β	B	β	B	β	B	β	B	β
Constant	.547		.547		.444		.543		.444	
	(.060)		(.061)		(.064)		(.061)		(.064)	
Population Density (ln)	-.027		-.027		-.025		-.027		-.025	
	(.003)	-.230**	(.003)	-.230**	(.003)	-.214**	(.003)	-.230**	(.003)	-.214**
Median Age of Males	.004		.004		.003		.004		.003	
	(.001)	.085**	(.001)	.086**	(.001)	.071**	(.001)	.084**	(.001)	.071**
Percent born in South	-.001		-.001		.000		-.001		.000	
	(.000)	-.184**	(.000)	-.184**	(.000)	-.096**	(.000)	-.179**	(.000)	-.094**
Population Turnover	.002		.002		.003		.002		.003	
	(.001)	.092**	(.001)	.091**	(.001)	.132**	(.001)	.094**	(.001)	.133**
Voter turnout	.002		.002		.002		.002		.002	
	(.000)	.133**	(.000)	.132**	(.000)	.133**	(.000)	.131**	(.000)	.131**
Percent Divorced	.006		.006		.010		.007		.010	
	(.002)	.069**	(.002)	.069**	(.002)	.115**	(.002)	.076**	(.002)	.118**
Disadvantage Index	-.072		-.072		-.073		-.073		-.073	
	(.004)	-.491**	(.004)	-.490**	(.004)	-.495**	(.004)	-.492**	(.004)	-.496**
Percent Unemployed (ln)	-.024		-.024		-.019		-.022		-.018	
	(.013)	-.050	(.013)	-.050	(.013)	-.040	(.013)	-.047	(.013)	-.038

Table 6.4: OLS Coefficients: Suicide-Homicide Proportion on Control Variables and Measures of Religious Denominational Differences (continued)

Variable	4		5		6		7		8	
	B	β	B	β	B	β	B	β	B	β
Percent Religiously	.00005		.00004		.000		.0000574		.000	
Affiliated	(.000)	.004	(.000)	.004	(.000)	.043	(.000)	.005	(.000)	.042
Congregations per	.000		.000		.001		.000		.001	
100,000 residents	(.000)	.138**	(.000)	.137**	(.000)	.196**	(.000)	.142**	(.000)	.196**
Religious Homogeneity	-.005		-.005		.041		-.005		.041	
	(.025)	-.005	(.026)	-.004	(.027)	.039	(.025)	-.005	(.027)	.039
Evangelical			.000						.000	
			(.001)	.004					(.001)	.004
Fundamentalist					-.002				-.002	
					(.000)	-.184**			(.000)	-.181**
Pentecostal							-.002		-.001	
							(.002)	-.025	(.002)	-.015
Adjusted R^2	.648		.648		.655		.648		.654	

Note: Numbers in parentheses are standard errors. * $p < .05$ for a 2-tailed test; ** $p < .01$ for a 2-tailed test

SUICIDE-HOMICIDE PROPORTION

As with homicide, above, the only measure of denominational difference that impacts the SHP is percent fundamentalist Protestant. The fundamentalist variable influences the SHP as hypothesized, both when examined alone in model 6 (β = -.184), and along with evangelicals and Pentecostals in model 8 (β = -.181). Consequently, table 6.4 (below), models 6 and 8 taken together show that increases in percent fundamentalist Protestant result in higher proportions of county-level lethal violence manifesting as homicide as opposed to suicide. Furthermore, the percent born in the South loses nearly half of its effect and the effect of percent divorced nearly doubles when fundamentalist Protestants are included in the model.

INTERACTION TERM

Shifting the focus to model III, which examines the expectation of an interaction between religious institutional effects and religious denominational effects, model 9 in table 6.5 (below) shows that the interaction between religious homogeneity and percent fundamentalist Protestant is not significant. Similarly, model 9, Table 6.6 (below), shows no significant relationship between the interaction term and county homicide rates. Moreover, no statistically significant relationship was found either between the interaction term and the lethal violence rate (model 9, table 6.7 below) or the SHP (model 9, table 6.8 below). Furthermore, tests of the interactions between congregations per 100,000 and percent fundamentalist Protestant revealed similarly non-significant effects for each of the four dependent variables.

Table 6.5: OLS Coefficients: Suicide Rates on the mean centered product term.

Variable	8		9	
	B	β	B	β
Constant	-5.129 (1.871)		-7.050 (1.834)	
Population Density (ln)	-.861 (.088)	-.303**	-.892 (.089)	-.314**
Median Age of Males	.308 (.029)	.301**	.311 (.029)	.304**
Percent Born in South	.007 (.004)	.073	.010 (.004)	.098*
Population Turnover	.097 (.016)	.195**	.098 (.016)	.195**
Voter turnout	-.040 (.014)	-.092**	-.042 (.014)	-.096**
Percent Divorced	.834 (.060)	.388**	.836 (.060)	.389**
Disadvantage Index	-.097 (.114)	-.027	-.085 (.114)	-.024
Percent Unemployed (ln)	1.309 (.373)	.112**	1.282 (.373)	.109**
Percent Religiously Affiliated	.027 (.008)	.100**	.029 (.008)	.108**
Congregations per 100,000 residents	.006 (.002)	.084*	.004 (.002)	.062
Religious Homogeneity	-4.633 (.800)	-.178**	-4.553 (.800)	-.175**
Evangelical	-.002 (.028)	-.001	-.002 (.028)	-.001
Fundamentalist	.003 (.013)	.013	-.013 (.015)	-.048
Pentecostal	.128 (.057)	.057*	.130 (.056)	.057*
Fundamentalist x religious homogeneity			.096 (.052)	.065
Adjusted R^2	.504		.505	

Note: Numbers in parentheses are standard errors.
* $p < .05$ for a 2-tailed test; ** $p < .01$ for a 2-tailed test

Table 6.6: OLS Coefficients: Homicide Rates (ln) on the mean centered product term.

Variable	8		9	
	B	β	B	β
Constant	1.645 (.269)		1.539 (.264)	
Population Density (ln)	.053 (.013)	.113**	.054 (.013)	.116**
Median Age of Males	.005 (.004)	.029	.005 (.004)	.028
Percent born in South	.003 (.001)	.165**	.003 (.001)	.159**
Population Turnover	-.006 (.002)	-.069*	-.006 (.002)	-.069*
Voter turnout	-.012 (.002)	-.173**	-.012 (.002)	-.172**
Percent Divorced	.024 (.009)	.067**	.024 (.009)	.067**
Disadvantage Index	.269 (.016)	.453**	.269 (.016)	.452**
Percent Unemployed (ln)	.136 (.054)	.070*	.137 (.054)	.071*
Percent Religiously Affiliated	.000 (.001)	-.009	.000 (.001)	-.011
Congregations per 100,000 residents	-.002 (.000)	-.153**	-.002 (.000)	-.148**
Religious Homogeneity	-.480 (.115)	-.112**	-.484 (.115)	-.113**
Evangelical	-.002 (.004)	-.010	-.002 (.004)	-.010
Fundamentalist	.009 (.002)	.198**	.009 (.002)	.214**
Pentecostal	.014 (.008)	.037	.014 (.008)	.036
Fundamentalist x religious homogeneity			-.004 (.007)	-.016
Adjusted R^2	.624		.623	

Note: Numbers in parentheses are standard errors.
* $p < .05$ for a 2-tailed test; ** $p < .01$ for a 2-tailed test

Table 6.7: OLS Coefficients: Lethal Violence Rates on the mean centered product term.

Variable	8		9	
	B	β	B	β
Constant	-1.802		-4.579	
	(2.917)		(2.862)	
Population Density (ln)	-.349		-.388	
	(.137)	-.079*	(.139)	-.087**
Median Age of Males	.298		.301	
	(.046)	.186**	(.046)	.188**
Percent born in South	.020		.023	
	(.006)	.131**	(.007)	.151**
Population Turnover	.073		.073	
	(.026)	.093**	(.026)	.093**
Voter turnout	-.067		-.070	
	(.022)	-.099**	(.022)	-.103**
Percent Divorced	.941		.944	
	(.093)	.280**	(.093)	.281**
Disadvantage Index	2.371		2.386	
	(.178)	.421**	(.178)	.424**
Percent Unemployed (ln)	2.086		2.052	
	(.582)	.114**	(.582)	.112**
Percent Religiously Affiliated	.023		.025	
	(.012)	.054*	(.012)	.060*
Congregations per 100,000 residents	.000		-.001	
	(.004)	.003	(.004)	-.014
Religious Homogeneity	-7.535		-7.436	
	(1.247)	-.186**	(1.248)	-.183**
Evangelical	.035		.035	
	(.044)	.019	(.044)	.019
Fundamentalist	.036		.016	
	(.020)	.088	(.024)	.039
Pentecostal	.129		.131	
	(.088)	.037	(.088)	.037
Fundamentalist x religious			.119	
homogeneity			(.081)	.051
Adjusted R^2	.506		.507	

Note: Numbers in parentheses are standard errors.
* p < .05 for a 2-tailed test; ** p < .01 for a 2-tailed test

Table 6.8: OLS Coefficients: Suicide-Homicide Proportion on the mean centered product term.

Variable	**8**		**9**	
	B	**β**	**B**	**β**
Constant	.444 (.064)		.439 (.063)	
Population Density (ln)	-.025 (.003)	-.214**	-.025 (.003)	-.217**
Median Age of Males	.003 (.001)	.071**	.003 (.001)	.071**
Percent born in South	.000 (.000)	-.094**	.000 (.000)	-.088*
Population Turnover	.003 (.001)	.133**	.003 (.001)	.133**
Voter turnout	.002 (.000)	.131**	.002 (.000)	.129**
Percent Divorced	.010 (.002)	.118**	.010 (.002)	.119**
Disadvantage Index	-.073 (.004)	-.496**	-.073 (.004)	-.495**
Percent Unemployed (ln)	-.018 (.013)	-.038	-.018 (.013)	-.038
Percent Religiously Affiliated	.000 (.000)	.042	.000 (.000)	.044
Congregations per 100,000 residents	.001 (.000)	.196**	.001 (.000)	.191**
Religious Homogeneity	.041 (.027)	.039	.042 (.027)	.039
Evangelical	.000 (.001)	.004	.000 (.001)	.004
Fundamentalist	-.002 (.000)	-.181**	-.002 (.001)	-.197**
Pentecostal	-.001 (.002)	-.015	-.001 (.002)	-.015
Fundamentalist x religious homogeneity			.001 (.002)	.017
Adjusted R^2	.654		.654	

Note: Numbers in parentheses are standard errors.
* p < .05 for a 2-tailed test; ** p < .01 for a 2-tailed test

FURTHER ANALYSIS

The above tests of the denominational effects literature point to several important conclusions that will be discussed in this section. First, the standard practice of combining evangelical and fundamentalist Protestants into a single measure of conservative Protestants is worth questioning. Second, there is evidence to support the denominational effects model with regards to county-level homicide rates, but not suicide rates. Finally, the predicted interaction effect between denominational and institutional effects on lethal violence cannot be substantiated.

In alignment with Blanchard et al.'s (2008) assertion that substantial public health differences exist between evangelical communities on the one hand and fundamentalist and Pentecostal communities on the other hand, this study demonstrates that percent fundamentalist adversely affects county homicide rates while percent Pentecostal adversely affects county suicide rates. This fundamentalist effect, however, also supports Jensen's (2006) religious cosmologies hypothesis, which asserts that religious groups with dualist theologies and strong inerrancy doctrines encourage externalized lethal aggression throughout the community, a theory that predicts high homicide rates in such communities but predicts no effect on suicide rates.

The non-significant effects of two of the sub-branches of conservative Protestantism on suicide rates runs directly counter to the claims by Pescosolido and Georgianna (1989) that modern conservative Protestants generate networks, like those of Catholics, that should provide protective benefits from suicide. One possible explanation for the lack of protective effects against suicide from conservative Protestant presence in counties may be linked to the bonding social capital that they generate. Specifically, the protective effects of highly religious groups, particularly those that favor bonding social capital over bridging social capital, will only extend to the members of the religious groups. Consequently, highly conservative Protestant communities may fail to provide adequate networks for reducing overall county-level suicide since any beneficial social networks that they generate would be unlikely to extend beyond the church membership. On the other hand, as proposed in chapter 5, counties with strong mainline Protestant institutions may generate reduced suicide rates by providing bridging social networks that benefit both their members and the rest of the community.

Finally, before moving on to further analysis of the unexpected finding on suicide, it is important to note that the hypothesized interaction between religious institutional effects and religious denominational effects was not demonstrated by this analysis. While the lack of interaction between religious homogeneity (a force of production) and percent fundamentalist Protestant (a force of direction) does not disprove the integrated model, it does raise questions about its utility in this particular study.

Disaggregating Religious Affiliation

Given the persistent, albeit small, positive effect of percent religiously affiliated on the suicide rate, it is also worth investigating the hypothesis from chapter 5, that is, that the higher suicide rates associated with higher levels of religiosity may be occurring among religiously unaffiliated residents who may not benefit from social networks generated by those religious institutions which foster bonding social capital. As noted before, this idea is impossible to test directly without data on religious characteristics of decedents. Nevertheless, it is possible to assess whether the percentage of residents affiliated with bridging religious groups (i.e., mainline Protestant) impacts suicide rates differently than the percentage of residents affiliated with bonding religious groups (i.e., conservative Protestant). Similarly, the density of bridging congregations can be compared to that of bonding congregations by disaggregating congregations per 100,000 into denominational groupings. This second hypothesis may also be useful for further explaining the unexpected positive relationship between congregations per 100,000 and suicide, as well as the lack of significant relationship between conservative Protestant denominations and suicide.

Model 11 in table 6.9 (below) shows the importance of examining the disaggregated percentages of religious affiliation. Of particular interest is the significant negative relationship between percent mainline Protestant (β = -.127) and the suicide rate, which run countervailing to the significant positive effects of percent conservative Protestant (β = .132) and percent Catholic (β = .143) on county suicide rates. Model 12 in table 6.11 (below) also shows the impact of disaggregating the congregational groups on the trimmed suicide model derived from chapter 5. In this model, percent religiously affiliated appears non-significant, while religious homogeneity remains strongly and negatively correlated with suicide. Moreover, the number of mainline Protestant congregations per 100,000 residents ($\beta = -.103$) has a significant negative relationship with suicide while Catholic ($\beta = .128$) and conservative Protestant ($\beta = .215$) congregations per 100,000 both have significant positive relationships with the suicide rate.

Further investigation using a test for nonlinear effects (see Table 6.10 below) indicates that a nonlinear relationship exists between the percent mainline Protestant affiliated and the suicide rate. In particular, it appears that suicide rates decline initially as percent mainline Protestant affiliated increases but, as counties reach roughly twenty percent mainline Protestant, suicide rates begin increasing as the mainline Protestant population rises (see Figure 6.1 below). A closer look at the sample of counties chosen shows the mean percentage of mainline Protestant affiliated as 10.98 percent, with the lowest percentage 0.19 in Utah County, Utah and the highest at 45.32 in Goodhue County, Minnesota. In fact, slightly more than 90 percent of the counties included in this study have mainline Protestant affiliated populations of less than 20 percent. However, low levels of mainline Protestant participation in the counties included in this study are consistent with low levels found throughout the country, where the mean percentage of mainline Protestant adherents is 14.2 percent, and roughly 80 percent of all US counties have mainline Protestant affiliated populations of less than 20 percent. Consequently, the unexpected finding of a negative relationship between the presence of mainline Protestant populations and suicide seems due to the relatively small numbers of counties with mainline Protestant majorities. It is also worth noting that while percent conservative Protestant adherents shows no evidence of nonlinearity, the percentage of Catholic adherents does show a similar curvilinear effect on suicide rates to that of mainline Protestants.

Table 6.9: OLS Coefficients: Suicide Rates on Denominational Specific Measures of Institutional Strength of Religion.

Variable	8		11		12	
	B	β	B	β	B	β
Constant	-5.488		-2.823		-4.073	
	(1.756)		(1.836)		(1.793)	
Population Density (ln)	-.857		-.818		-.758	
	(.087)	-.302**	(.088)	-.287**	(.090)	-.267**
Median Age of Males	.304		.321		.351	
	(.029)	.297**	(.030)	.314**	(.029)	.343**
Percent Born in South	.009		.009		.010	
	(.003)	.092**	(.004)	.090*	(.003)	.100**
Population Turnover	.102		.085		.078	
	(.016)	.203**	(.016)	.170**	(.016)	.157**
Voter turnout	-.042		-.038		-.051	
	(.014)	-.097**	(.014)	-.089**	(.014)	-.117**
Percent Divorced	.874		.776		.769	
	(.053)	.406**	(.060)	.361**	(.056)	.358**
Disadvantage Index	-.108		-.085		-.125	
	(.114)	-.030	(.127)	-.016	(.113)	-.035
Percent Unemployed	1.407		.714		.839	
(ln)	(.371)	.120**	(.384)	.061	(.373)	.072*
Percent Religiously	.028				-.004	
Affiliated	(.007)	.104**			(.008)	-.015
Congregations per	.006		.013			
100,000 residents	(.002)	.096**	(.003)	.194**		
Religious Homogeneity	-4.556		-6.886		-4.772	
	(.738)	-.175**	(.970)	-.265**	(.848)	-.184**
Percent Mainline			-.073			
Protestant			(.016)	-.127**		
Percent Conservative			.033			
Protestant			(.011)	.132**		
Percent Catholic			.035			
			(.010)	.143**		

Table 6.9: OLS Coefficients: Suicide Rates on Denominational Specific Measures of Institutional Strength of Religion (continued)

Variable	8		11		12	
	B	β	B	β	B	β
Percent Other			.001			
			(.011)	-.002		
Mainline Protestant						
Congregations per					-.015	
100,000 residents					(.004)	-.103**
Conservative Protestant						
Congregations per					.017	
100,000 residents					(.003)	.215**
Catholic Congregations					.064	
per 100,000 residents					(.017)	.128**
Other Congregations					.025	
per 100,000 residents					(.005)	.121**
Adjusted R^2	.503		.514		.523	

Note: Numbers in parentheses are standard errors.
* p < .05 for a 2-tailed test; ** p < .01 for a 2-tailed test

Table 6.10: OLS Coefficients from the Polynomial Regression of Suicide Rates on Denominational Specific Measures of Institutional Strength of Religion.

Variable	11		13	
	B	β	B	β
Constant	-2.823		-.650	
	(1.836)		(1.912)	
Population Density (ln)	-.818		-.702	
	(.088)	-.287**	(.093)	-.246**
Median Age of Males	.321		.336	
	(.030)	.314**	(.029)	.329**
Percent Born in South	.009		.007	
	(.004)	.090*	(.004)	.069
Population Turnover	.085		.075	
	(.016)	.170**	(.016)	.150**
Voter turnout	-.038		-.031	
	(.014)	-.089**	(.014)	-.072*
Percent Divorced	.776		.738	
	(.060)	.361**	(.059)	.343**
Disadvantage Index	-.085		.101	
	(.127)	-.016	(.129)	.028
Percent Unemployed (ln)	.714		.372	
	(.384)	.061	(.383)	.032
Congregations per 100,000 residents	.013		.016	
	(.003)	.194**	(.004)	.249**
Religious Homogeneity	-6.886		-9.171	
	(.970)	-.265**	(1.074)	-.353**
Percent Mainline Protestant	-.073		-.291	
	(.016)	-.127**	(.048)	-.505**
Percent Conservative Protestant	.033		.055	
	(.011)	.132**	(.012)	.218**
Percent Catholic	.035		-.03	
	(.010)	.143**	(.021)	-.121
Percent Other	.001		-.029	
	(.011)	-.002	(.012)	-.082*
Percent Mainline Protestant^2			.007	
			(.001)	.360**
Percent Conservative Protestant^2			-.000	
			(.000)	-.070
Percent Catholic^2			.001	
			(.000)	.280**
Adjusted R^2	.514		.529	

Note: Numbers in parentheses are standard errors.
* $p < .05$ for a 2-tailed test; ** $p < .01$ for a 2-tailed test

Figure 6.1: Graph of Nonlinear Relationship Between Percent Mainline Affiliated and County Suicide Rates.

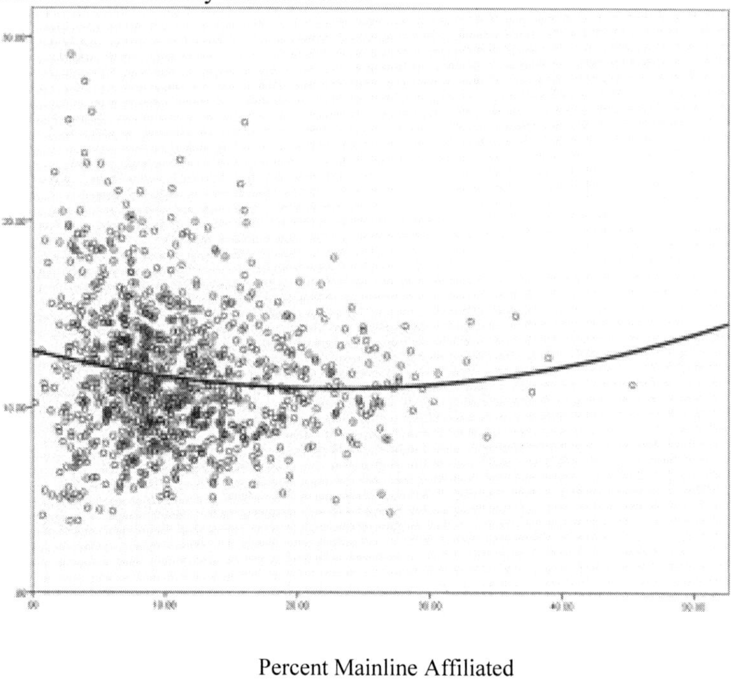

CHAPTER 7:

Conclusions

The goal of this study was to explore the utility of the integrated model of lethal violence in regards to understanding religion's influence on homicide and suicide. In general, the integrated model departs from traditional approaches to lethal violence by focusing on the interplay between homicide rates and suicide rates as opposed to viewing them as independent phenomena. Unnithan et al.'s (1994) original formulation of the integrated model divides variables affecting lethal violence into two categories: (1) those that increase lethal violence (forces of production) and (2) those that channel lethal violence internally toward suicide or externally toward homicide (forces of direction). This chapter's purpose is to assess to what extent the integrated model is capable of advancing our understanding of religion's role in county-level lethal violence rates. The first section of this chapter will briefly review the findings reported in chapters 5 and 6. The second section will discuss how the details of the findings inform each of the several theoretical models linking religion and lethal violence. The third section will address limitations of this research, and the final section will suggest directions for future study of religion and lethal violence.

KEY FINDINGS

One of the potential benefits of employing the integrated model to address religion's effect on lethal violence is the model's ability to provide an "umbrella" framework under which the two major theoretical approaches to religion's impact on lethal violence can be joined together. By bringing together two separate literatures, one focused on the structural impacts of religion on the production of lethal violence (i.e., institutional effects) and one focused on the cultural impacts of religion on the direction of lethal violence (i.e., denominational effects), it was possible to assess the utility of the integrated model and gain insights into each model individually. In reviewing chapters 5 and 6, this section will first present the findings for the institutional effects model, then the findings for the denominational effects model, and lastly, the findings for the integrated model.

The Institutional Effects Model

Attempts to determine the impact of religion as an institution on violence rates can be traced back to Durkheim and early moral statisticians Guerrry, Morselli and Ferri. Historically, scholars have asserted that religion as an institution should logically provide protective effects against lethal violence in society. Prior research in this area has been fragmented as to both how to operationalize the institutional strength of religion and whether or not to focus on suicide or homicide. The present study addresses this fragmentation by employing three measures of religious institutional strength (i.e., percent religiously affiliated, congregations per 100,000 residents, and the Simpson/Herfindahl index of religious homogeneity) to examine the incidence of both homicide and suicide independently and in combination. Although each of these measures has been used independently in prior studies, they each address different ways of thinking about religious institutional strength within a community. Religious affiliation and congregational density, for example, focus on the pervasiveness of religion within a community by drawing attention to the proportion of the community connected to religious institutions and the number of religious institutions available to the community. Religious homogeneity, on the other hand, focuses attention on the extent to which the religious community within a county is unified under the same religious tradition. Using these three measures of institutional strength, each of the following hypotheses was investigated:

1) Community suicide rates will be inversely correlated with the strength of community religious institutions.

2) Community homicide rates will be inversely correlated with the strength of community religious institutions.
3) Community lethal violence rates will be inversely correlated with the strength of community religious institutions.
4) The suicide-homicide proportion will not be significantly correlated with the strength of community religious intuitions.

In general, each of these hypotheses was supported when institutional strength was measured by the Simpson/Herfindahl index of homogeneity, but the results were mixed when congregational density or percent religiously affiliated were used as the measure of religious institutional strength.

Suicide. Surprisingly, only one of the three measures of religious institutional strength operated as hypothesized with regards to the suicide rate. Confirming earlier findings reported at the city level by Ellision et al. (1997), religious homogeneity appears to curtail county suicide rates. Conversely, both percent religiously affiliated and congregations per 100,000 residents were associated with higher suicide rates. Further analysis investigated the possibility of an interaction between religious homogeneity and the percent religiously affiliated. When religious affiliation is high, higher levels of religious homogeneity result in lower suicide rates, but when religious affiliation is low, higher levels of religious homogeneity result in higher suicide rates. This finding suggests that Stark's moral communities hypothesis, which suggests that higher rates of religiosity alone should serve to reduce community anti-social behavior, needs to be modified. In particular, these findings reveal that the homogeneity of religious communities also matters. As Stark and Bainbridge (1996) predicted, small pockets of religious groups have little impact on reducing suicide but, contrary to their predictions, neither does widespread religious participation in religiously fragmented counties. *Moral communities do, however, seem to reduce suicide rates in counties marked by both high rates of religiosity and high levels of religious homogeneity.*

Homicide. Although the percent religiously affiliated showed no relationship with the homicide rates of counties, both congregations per 100,000 residents and religious homogeneity contribute to lower homicide rates. These findings support and expand both Stark and Bainbridge's (1996) moral communities hypothesis and Lee's (2006) research on the role of religious institutions in reducing crime. These results, however, highlight that the presence of religious institutions and the unified nature of those institutions are far more important in reducing homicide rates than is the percentage of religiously affiliated residents in a community. This understanding of the institutional effects of religion on homicide also brings into question the assumption by early moral community theorists that the number of believers in a community was far more important than what they believed. In other words, it is not the case that all religious communities are equal in their ability to resist homicide but, rather, that *religiously homogenous communities and communities dense with religious institutions are more resistant to homicide than are communities that are secular, religiously heterogeneous, or sparsely populated with churches, temples, and synagogues.*

Lethal Violence. As with the disaggregated homicide and suicide rates, lethal violence rates were negatively correlated with the county's level of religious homogeneity. Contrary to the hypothesized effects, the percent religiously affiliated was positively correlated with lethal violence rates, but there was no relationship between lethal violence and the number of congregations per 100,000 residents. It is worth noting that while only the effect of religious homogeneity is in line with the theoretical expectations of the institutional effects hypothesis, all of the findings on lethal violence rates do follow logically from the findings on suicide and homicide. For example, the positive relationship between percent religiously affiliated and lethal violence could easily be derived arithmetically by adding the positive relationship between percent religiously affiliated and suicide to the non-significant relationship between percent religiously affiliated and homicide. Similar logic can also be applied to the positive relationship between congregational density and suicide combined with the negative relationship between congregational density and homicide, resulting in no relationship for the combined variables. Also, the negative relationships between religious homogeneity and both suicide and homicide logically result in a negative relationship with lethal violence as a whole.

Suicide-Homicide Proportion. The hypothesized absence of an effect of religious affiliation and religious homogeneity on the SHP was confirmed, but a positive relationship between congregational density and the SHP implies that large numbers of congregations in a county contribute to lethal violence rates shifting toward suicide and away from homicide. This finding, while contrary to the hypothesized effect, can also be logically deduced from the individual findings on homicide and suicide which indicate that congregations per capita is positively correlated with suicide and negatively correlated with homicide, which are the components of the suicide/homicide proportion.

The Denominational Effects Model

Although historically research on denominational effects focused primarily on differences between Catholics and Protestants, modern scholarship has begun to investigate the significant differences between conservative and mainline Protestants. The present research draws on the commonalities between the suicide and homicide literatures' explanations of how mainline and conservative Protestants differ in their influence on lethal violence rates.

5) Community suicide rates will be inversely correlated with the proportion of the community that is affiliated with conservative Protestant denominations.
6) Community homicide rates will be positively correlated with the proportion of the community that is affiliated with conservative Protestant denominations.
7) Community lethal violence rates will not be significantly correlated with the proportion of the community that is affiliated with conservative Protestant denominations.
8) Community suicide-homicide proportion will be inversely correlated with the proportion of the community that is affiliated with conservative Protestant denominations.

Suicide. No support for hypothesis one was found in this research. While both fundamentalists and evangelicals showed no relationship with county suicide rates, the presence of Pentecostals was actually positively correlated with the suicide rate. This finding does partially confirm Blanchard et al.'s (2008) claim that significant differences exist among the different subgroups of conservative Protestantism. However, they suggest that the focus on bonding social capital and otherworldly issues by fundamentalists and Pentecostals results in weakened public health structures in their communities, which in turn leads to higher mortality rates from limited health care access. Blanchard et al. further suggest that by focusing on bridging social capital, evangelicals, like mainline Protestants and Catholics, should contribute to stronger public health systems for their communities leading to lower mortality rates. With regards to the present findings, it appears that *Pentecostals and fundamentalist Protestants do adversely impact the suicide rates in the case of the former and homicide rates in the case of the latter*. Furthermore, evangelicals have no effect on either form of lethal violence. While these findings are consistent with the notion that important differences exist between subgroups of conservative Protestants, it does not appear that weakened public health infrastructures are the vehicle through which these differences manifest, as each sub-group impacts homicide and suicide differently.

Homicide. Hypothesis two was supported when examining the prevalence of fundamentalist Protestants. *With the exception of disadvantage, the percent fundamentalist Protestant was the second strongest predictor of county homicide rates*. However, neither the presence of evangelicals nor the presence of Pentecostals had an impact on the homicide rates.

Lethal Violence. Hypothesis three was confirmed as none of the three sub-branches of conservative Protestantism appeared correlated with the lethal violence rate of counties.

Suicide-Homicide Proportion. Hypothesis four was partially supported since fundamentalist Protestants were inversely related to the SHP, but neither of the other two subgroups showed any relationship with the SHP.

The Integrated Model

Following the logic presented by Unnithan et al., it was hypothesized that an interaction should exist between the measures of religious institutional strength and the denominational measures. In particular, the preventive effect of religious homogeneity on homicide rates should be attenuated in counties with high percentages of fundamentalist Protestants, while the preventive effect of religious homogeneity on suicide rates should be amplified in counties with high percentages of fundamentalist Protestants. However, a *test of the interaction effect between community religiosity and the proportion of externalizing denominations revealed no significant effect.*

DISCUSSION

The overarching question to be answered by this study is whether or not anything can be gained by applying Unnithan et al.'s integrated model to an investigation of religious effects on lethal violence. To begin to answer that question, this section will first address the overall success of the integrated model in explaining religion's role in county-level violence. Next will follow a discussion of the utility of applying the model with regards to bridging different theoretical traditions and identifying variables of theoretical interest. Finally, this section will discuss at length some of the theoretical and empirical problems inherent in the Unnithan et al.'s integrated model.

The Integrated Model (Support for)

Little overall support for the integrated model was found by this analysis. Within the framework of institutional effects, only unemployment and religious homogeneity clearly operated as forces of production, while, contrary to theoretical predictions, congregational density acted as a force of direction. Similarly, percent religiously affiliated appeared to act counter to predictions by increasing the lethal violence rate, but only through its impact on suicide. Furthermore, each control variable, with the exception of the aforementioned unemployment rate, appears to be acting as both a force of production and force of direction. Finally, the lack of a significant interaction effect between religious institutional strength and denominational composition further demonstrates the unlikelihood that the stream model is the best fit for understanding religion's impact on lethal violence.

The Integrated Model (Utility of)

While there is little evidence for the integrated model considered as a whole, it is worth distinguishing between two major components of the integrated model -- namely, the aggregated approach to lethal violence, and the stream model. The former component is the claim originated by early moral statisticians that there are commonalties between homicide and suicide that make examining one in conjunction with the other a worthwhile endeavor. The latter component is Unnithan et al.'s contribution to the integrated model, in which they argue that lethal violence not only shares similar forces of production, but that a second level of variables exists that conditions the outcome of the violence (i.e., forces of direction). While the stream model appears less than ideal for addressing religion's role in lethal violence, there is still value in theorizing about the role of religion in lethal violence that may not be achieved by examining religion's role in either homicide or suicide considered alone.

Prior research on homicide, for example, has completely overlooked the role of religious homogeneity. Since the integrated model directs us to closely consider any correlate of suicide as a possible correlate of homicide and *vice versa*, then prior research identifying homogeneity as a factor in suicide rates indicates that a link between homogeneity and homicide may be worth exploring. During this research a significant negative correlation between religious homogeneity and homicide emerged. While prior research on the institutional effects of religion on homicide focused exclusively on congregational density, religious homogeneity appears to play an equally important role in minimizing homicide rates. Moreover, religious homogeneity appears to be of broader significance than congregational density since it directly impacts both homicide and suicide rates. Consequently, *homogeneity provides a greater net benefit than the other measures of religious institutional strength.*

The link between religious homogeneity and both types of lethal violence makes theoretical sense. First, religiously uniform counties benefit from a reduced number of competing interests that may impede the development of a strong public health system. As Blanchard et al. (2008) point out, different religious traditions hold different views about the role medicine in an individual's life. Consequently, religious heterogeneity in a community may mire the public health system in debates ranging from the ethics of birth control to medical intervention. Second, religious uniformity should work to make the differences in bridging and bonding social capital less relevant since this distinction relies heavily on the existence of an in-group and an out-group within the community. Consequently, as the community becomes more homogenous, especially along such polarizing and divisive lines as religion, bridging social capital plays less of a role since there are fewer groups to bridge between. Similarly, in homogenous counties bonding social capital can serve the needs of the entire community as there are few "others" for bonding social capital to exclude.

Interestingly, it appears that more secular communities can still benefit from smaller but homogenous religious communities in regards to keeping homicide rates low. However, with regards to suicide, the interaction between percent religiously affiliated and religious homogeneity demonstrates that protective effect of religious homogeneity is attenuated in highly religious communities. Finally, the significance of religious homogeneity uncovered here also aligns well with social disorganization theory which has theorized that homogeneity, usually conceptualized with reference to ethnic or racial categories (Sampson and Groves 1989), may play a role in community crime rates. Consequently, a broader understanding of homogeneity that incorporates religion may help inform the social disorganization literature in new ways.

The Integrated Model (Critique)

One particular problem that arises when taking Unnithan et al.'s approach is the difficulty in finding mutually exclusive variables that clearly operate as forces of direction or forces of production, but not as both. Based on Wu's (2003; 2004) concerns, efforts were made to carefully categorize each variable in this study as a force of production or a force of direction based on theory. However, results demonstrate empirically that many of these concepts operate as both forces of direction and forces of production (i.e., population density, median age of males, percent born in South, population turnover, voter turnout, percent divorced and the disadvantage index).

Another problem generated by Unnithan et al.'s integrated model arises when one considers the time order expectations of the theory to the time order of real life lethal events. At its core the stream theory assumes that forces of production first frustrate an individual, creating the potential for violence, and then separate forces of direction influence the individual to externalize or internalize the violence. But scholars examining violence at the individual level have argued that interpersonal violence, such as homicide, is often the result of a series of exchanges between victim and offender where the victim's actions and words both simultaneously frustrate the offender and direct the consequences of the frustration his or her way (Felson and Steadman 1983; Luckenbill 1977; Wolfgang 1958). Moreover, with suicides, the force of production and force of direction may both arise from an individual's frustration with his or her own perceived failings. Given this understanding of lethal violence, it becomes difficult to apply the stream model of lethal violence since the force of production (frustration) and force of direction (in this case, the source of frustration) are one and the same, and present themselves simultaneously. In these cases, however, the integrated model's assumption that homicide and suicide share at least some similar dynamics is still relevant since both frustrating events (such as job loss and divorce) and protective factors (such as political participation and religiosity) may play similar roles in determining suicide and homicide risk.

LIMITATIONS

Data for this research were collected from three primary sources: the Religious Congregations & Membership 2000, National Vital Statistics System (1999-2002) and the 2000 U.S. Census. As with any secondary analysis, data availability and reliability are two critical factors. The present study is no exception. This section will discuss case suppression, data integrity, and counties as a unit of analysis as three key limitations to the research.

Suppressed Data: One limitation of the present research is the focus on the one third most densely populated counties in order to avoid suppressed data in the vital statistics record. Because of this limited focus on counties with larger populations, very little can be inferred about religion's impact in rural counties. Since structural and cultural differences exist between rural and urban counties that may significantly affect lethal violence rates (Faupel, Kowalski, and Starr 1987; Kowalski and Duffield 1990; Kowalski, Faupel, and Starr 1987), it is highly likely that religion may play significantly different roles in small rural communities than in large urban or suburban communities. For example, religious homogeneity may play an even more important role in rural counties given the higher intensity of religious commitment and participation reported in smaller communities (Putnam and Campbell 2010). The stronger intensity of religion in rural communities could serve to intensify the effects of religion through the production of stronger and denser social networks. It is also possible that small counties may rely less on religious homogeneity to resist lethal violence since secular institutions in those counties may be more effective at unifying the community than they are in larger counties. Specifically, counties that are defined by a single school district or a major employer may find the social capital generated through the parent-teacher association or a local union, and the institutional strength of these organizations, suffice to reduce the risk of lethal violence independently of religion. Burkett and White (1974) first identified this problem, the anti-ascetic hypothesis, by pointing out that religion's prohibition on serious delinquency is not unique since many other social institutions also discourage the use of violence. Consequently, religious affiliation's influence on lethal violence may not manifest itself unless other social institutions are weak enough to fail at preventing violence. In a sense, the anti-ascetic hypothesis may play an important role in smaller counties if secular institutions are indeed stronger within these communities than in their more urbanized and suburban counterparts.

Unreliability of Data: As was discussed at length in chapter 4, there is a great deal of concern over the validity of homicide and suicide data collection methods in the United States. Although many of these concerns have been at least partially addressed, there are good reasons to be cautious when considering findings drawn from the official lethal violence data. With particular regards to suicide and religion, some scholars have raised the concern that community religiosity may play a role in the misclassification of suicides. For example, Day (1987) points out that the social construction of suicide rates can be tightly integrated with the religious affiliation of a community. Day suggests that lower rates of suicide among Catholics may indeed be a product of the resistance of Catholics to label a death as suicide due to the strong stigma attached to suicides by the Catholic Church. While the present study does not focus on Catholics, it is possible that stronger ideological opposition to suicide among conservative Protestants than mainline Protestants (Agnew 1998; Burdette, Hill, and Moulton 2005) may lead to similar discrepancies in death categorization within more politicized coroners' offices.

Units of Analysis: Although the focus on counties as a unit of analysis is a major advancement over many of the prior integrated model studies that have focused on larger units such as states and countries, there are a few tradeoffs involved with county-level data. First, counties lack any geographical uniformity, ranging in size from the 330,074 square miles of Alaska's Unorganized Borough to the 13 square miles of Hawaii's Kalawao County. This high degree of variability in the geographic size of counties raises questions about the comparability of the units. Second, variability between how counties determine causes of death can be problematic since many counties rely on elected coroners instead of formally trained medical examiners for this process. Finally, while counties often do provide a natural boundary for religious organizations which, like governments and secular groups often operate primarily within county borders, mega churches (those with 2,000 or more members) present a challenge since they often draw members from nearby counties making it difficult to identify their effects given that they transcend county borders.

FUTURE DIRECTIONS

Longitudinal Analysis

With the recent release of the 2010 Religious Congregations and Membership data, it seems reasonable for future research to address some of the longitudinal questions that revolve around religion and lethal violence. With longitudinal data it may be possible to investigate reciprocal effects between religion and lethal violence. For example, increasing rates of lethal violence in a county may expedite the out-migration of some religious groups as they seek less volatile areas, which in turn may impact the levels of religious homogeneity in a county. Similarly, increased lethal violence rates may also have an impact on religious homogeneity as fear of violence and violent victimization may both impact individual religious ideologies. Longitudinal data would also afford an opportunity to observe any lagged effects of institutional changes on county lethal violence rates. Since institutional changes seldom happen overnight, it may take years before shifts in community religious structures show any demonstrable effect on lethal violence rates.

Expanded Sample

With special permission from the National Center for Health Statistics, lethal violence counts for every county are available. An expanded analysis that examines all U.S. counties could be conducted, allowing for better understanding of the differences between rural and urban communities. Moreover, the expanded data would provide access to the large number of counties with homicide and suicide rates of zero, which may provide more insight into the protective effects of religion not available with the current data (which does not include any counties with less than ten lethal violence events).

Reevaluation of Integrated Model

Further theoretical reevaluation of the integrated model is also warranted given the mixed support uncovered here. What is to be made of variables that appear to be both forces of direction and forces of production? Unnithan et al. provide no guidance on this issue, and without clear and consistent guidelines regarding these components, the stream model may not be all that useful. Are there mechanisms other than frustration and attribution that operate as forces of production and forces of direction? Frustration, for example, seems to be only one of many possible motives for lethal violence, yet Unnithan et al. focus exclusively on various conceptualizations of frustration (e.g., poverty, inequality, etc.). In the present study, religion is conceptualized as a force of reduction, not production, by arguing that religious institutions have the power to stem the tide of lethal violence by reducing the flow of the stream. Future research, however, should look more closely into the role of secular institutions to ascertain if religious institutions are uniquely beneficial, symbiotically beneficial, or, as the anti-aesthetic hypothesis suggests, only necessary in the absence or failure of other institutions' strength. Similarly, the role of public health institutions within a county may play a significant role in reducing lethal violence by providing prevention campaigns, mental health resources, and medical intervention that may prevent a violent act from becoming lethal.

Likewise, Unnithan et al.'s focus on cultural differences in attribution as the explanatory force behind the SHP could also be augmented by considering other factors such as opportunity structures (Cohen and Felson 1979; Felson and Boba 2010; Miethe and Meier 1994) and situational factors (Felson and Steadman 1983; Luckenbill 1977; Wolfgang 1958) that may also operate as forces of direction. Finally, it is worthwhile to consider the broader impacts of theorizing about forces of production and forces of direction on deviance in general. For example, is it possible that religious homogeneity helps reduce rates of deviance in general, but that different denominations direct deviant behavior internally in the form of self-destructive deviance (e.g., drug use) or externally in the form of crimes against others (e.g., robbery).

CONCLUSION

In conclusion, it seems that early moral statisticians were correct to look for commonalities between homicide and suicide. By taking a broader look at the issue of lethal violence, homicide and suicide scholars can uncover causes of violence that were previously only examined by one literature or the other. In the case of religious homogeneity, Ellision et al.'s (1997) research on the role of religious homogeneity in reducing suicide had been ignored by homicide scholars, who continued the Durheimian tradition of theorizing and studying homicide and suicide as separate phenomena. Examining lethal violence through the lens of the integrated model, however, led to the discovery that religious homogeneity matters not just for suicide rates but for homicide rates as well. Unfortunately, Unithann et al.'s modern conceptualization of stream theory simply does not provide any additional explanatory power for religion's influence on lethal violence. Perhaps, with some further theoretical refinements, the stream model will produce more fruitful discoveries. Significantly, application of the integrated model here did uncover divergences between the way many scholars had theoretically conceptualized institutional strength of religion (as percent religiously affiliated or congregations per 100,000 residents) and how these two variables empirically operate with regards to homicide and suicide.

APPENDIX

Conservative Protestants by Congregations

Evangelical

- Allegheny Wesleyan Methodist Connection
- American Baptist Association
- Associate Reformed Presbyterian Church
- Christian Churches and Churches of Christ
- Christian Reformed Church in North America
- Cumberland Presbyterian Church
- Evangelical Presbyterian Church
- Association of Free Lutheran Congregations
- Free Methodist Church of North America
- Fundamental Methodist Conference, Inc.
- Lutheran Church – Missouri Synod
- Orthodox Presbyterian Church
- Presbyterian Church in America
- Primitive Methodist Church in the USA
- Seventh-day Adventist Church
- Wesleyan Church
- Wisconsin Evangelical Lutheran Synod

Fundamentalist

- Baptist General Conference
- Baptist Missionary Association of America
- Church of God (Anderson, Indiana)
- Church of the Nazarene
- Churches of Christ

- Conservative Baptist Association of America
- Duck River and Kindred Baptists Associations
- Enterprise Baptists Association
- National Association of Free Will Baptists
- General Six Principle Baptists
- Independent Free Will Baptists Associations
- Interstate & Foreign Landmark Missionary Baptists Association
- Jasper Baptist and Pleasant Valley Baptist Associations
- Landmark Missionary Baptists, Independent Associations and Unaffiliated Churches
- New Hope Baptist Association
- National Primitive Baptist Convention
- New Testament Association of Independent Baptist Churches and other Fundamental Baptist Associations/Fellowships
- Old Missionary Baptists Associations
- Original Free Will Baptists
- Primitive Baptist Churches – Old Line
- Primitive Baptist, Eastern District Association
- General Association of Regular Baptist Churches
- Reformed Baptist Churches
- Separate Baptists in Christ
- Southern Baptist Convention
- Southwide Baptist Fellowship
- Strict Baptists
- Two-seed-in-the-spirit predestination Baptists
- Wayne Trail Missionary Baptist Association

Pentecostal

- Assemblies of God
- Church of God (Cleveland, Tennessee)
- Church of God of Prophecy
- International Church of the Foursquare Gospel
- International Pentecostal Church of Christ
- Pentecostal Church of God
- International Pentecostal Holiness Church Vineyard, USA
- Independent, Charismatic Churches

References

Agnew, Robert. 1998. "The Approval of Suicide: A Social-Psychological Model." *Suicide and Life-Threatening Behavior* 28:205-225.

Akers, Ronald L. . 2010. "Religion and Crime." *The Criminologist: The Offical Newsletter of the American Society of Criminology* 35.

Albrecht, Stan L., Bruce A. Chadwick, and David S. Alcorn. 1977. "Religiosity and Deviance: Application of an Attitude-Behavior Contingent Consistency Model." *Journal for the Scientific Study of Religion* 16:263-274.

Applegate, Brandon K., Francis T. Cullen, Bonnie S. Fisher, and Thomas Vander Ven. 2000. "Forgiveness and Fundamentalism: Reconsidering the Relationship Between Correctional Attitudes and Religion." *Criminology* 38:719-754.

Baier, Colin J. and Bradley R. E. Wright. 2001. ""If You Love Me, Keep My Commandments": A Meta-Analysis of the Effect of Religion on Crime." *Journal of Research in Crime and Delinquency* 38:3-21.

Bainbridge, William Sims. 1989. "The Religious Ecology of Deviance." *Sociological Review* 54:288-295.

Baller, Robert D., Luc Anselin, Steven F. Messner, Glenn Deane, and Darnell F. Hawkins. 2001. "Structural Covariates of U.S. County Homicide Rates; Incorporating Spatial Effects." *Criminology* 39:561-590.

Batton, Candice. 2004. "Gender Differences in Lethal Violence: Historical Trends in the Relationship Between Homicide and Suicide Rates, 1960-2000." *Justice Quarterly* 21:423-461.

Batton, Candice and Robbin S. Ogle. 2003. ""Who's It Gonna Be--You or Me?" The Potential of Social Learning for Integrated Homicide-Suicide Theory." Pp. 85-108 in *Social Learning Theory and the Explanation of Crime: A Guide for the New Century*, edited by R. L. Akers and G. F. Jensen. Rutgers: Transaction Publishers.

Beeghley, Leonard. 2003. *Homicide: A Sociological Explanation*. Oxford: Rowman & Littlefield.

Benda, Brent B. and Robert Flynn Corwyn. 1997. "Religion and Delinquency: The Relationship after Considering Family and Peer Influences." *Journal for the Scientific Study of Religion* 36:81-92.

Benda, Brent B. and Nancy J. Toombs. 2000. "Religiosity and violence: Are they related after considering the strongest predictors?" *Journal of Criminal Justice* 28:483-496.

Beyerlein, Kraig and John R. Hipp. 2005. "Social Capital, Too Much of a Good Thing? American Religious Traditions and Community Crime." *Social Forces* 84:995-1013.

Bills, Corey B. and Guohua Li. 2005. "Correlating Homicide and Suicide." *International Journal of Epidemiology* 34:837-845.

Blanchard, Troy C. , John P. Bartkowski, Todd L. Matthews, and Kent R. Kerley. 2008. "Faith, Morality and Mortality: The Ecological Impact of Religion on Population Health." *Social Forces* 86:1591-1620.

Breault, K. D. . 1986. "Suicide in America: A Test of Durkheim's Theory of Religious and Family Integration, 1933--1980." *American Journal of Sociology* 92:628-656.

Bruce, Steve. 2011. "Defining religion: a practical response." *International Review of Sociology: Revue Internationale de Sociologie* 21:107-120.

Burdette, Amy M., Terrence D. Hill, and Benjamin E. Moulton. 2005. "Religion and Attitudes Toward Physician-Assisted Suicide and Terminal Palliative Care." *Journal for the Scientific Study of Religion* 44:79-93.

Burkett, Steven R. and Mervin White. 1974. "Hellfire and Delinquency: Another Look." *Journal for the Scientific Study of Religion* 13:455-462.

Centers for Disease Control and Prevention. 2012. "Surveillance for Violent Deaths -- National Violent Death Reporting System, 16 States, 2009." vol. 61, *Morbidity and Mortality Weekly Report.*

—. 2014. "Surveillance for Violent Deaths -- National Violent Death Reporting System, 16 States, 2010." vol. 63, *Morbidity and Mortality Weekly Report.*

Cerel, Julie, John R. Jordan, and Paul R. Duberstein. 2008. "The Impact of Suicide on the Family." *Crisis* 29:38-44.

Chaves, Mark. 2011. *Amercian Religion: Contemporary Trends*. Princeton: Princeton University Press.

Choldin, Harvey M. 1978. "Urban Density and Pathology." *Annual Review of Sociology* 4:91-113.

Chon, Don Soo. 2013. "Economic Development, Change of Age Distribution, and Stream Analogy of Homicide and Suicide: A Cross-National Assessment." *Justice Quarterly* 30:169-193.

Cohen, Lawrence E. and Marcus Felson. 1979. "Social Change and Crime Rate Trends: A Routine Activity Approach." *American Sociological Review* 44:588 - 608.

Cohen, Patricia, Judith S. Brook, Jacos Cohen, C. Noemi Velez, and Marc Garcia. 1990. "Common and uncommon pathways to adolescent psychopathology and problem behavior." Pp. 242-258 in *Straight and Devious Pathways from Childhood to Adulthood*, edited by L. Robins and M. Rutter. New York: Cambridge University Press.

Corso, Phaedra S., James A. Mercy, Thomas R. Simon, Eric A. Finkelstein, and Ted R. Miller. 2007. "Medical Costs and Productivity Losses Due to Interpersonal and Self-Directed Violence in the United States." *American Journal of Preventive Medicine* 32:474-482.

Cretacci, Michael A. 2003. "Religion and Social Control: An Application of a Modified Social Bond on Violence." *Criminal Justice Review* 28:254-277.

Cullen, Francis T. 2010. "Toward a criminology of religion: comment on Johnson and Jang." Pp. 151-161 in *American Society of Criminology 2010 Conference*, edited by R. Rosenfeld, K. Quinet, and C. Garcia. San Francisco, CA: Wadsworth.

Cutlip, Anna C., William B. Bankston, and Matthew R. Lee. 2010. "Civic Community and Nonmetropolitan White Suicide." *Archives of Suicide Research* 14:261-265.

Dahlberg, Linda L. and James A. Mercy. 2009. "History of Violence as a Public Health Problem." *American Medical Association Journal of Ethics* 11:167-172.

Day, Lincoln H. 1987. "Durkheim on Religion and Suicide -- A Demographic Critique." *Sociology* 21:449-461.

Desmond, Scott A., George Kikuchi, and Kristopher H. Morgan. 2010. "Congregations and Crime: Is the Spatial Distribution of Congregations Associated with Neighborhood Crime Rates?" *Journal for the Scientific Study of Religion* 49:37-55.

DiIulio, Jr., John J. 2009. "More Religion, Less Crime? Science, Felonies, and the Three Faith Factors." *Annual Review of Law and Social Sciences* 5:115-133.

Douglas, Jack D. 1967. *The Social Meanings of Suicide*. Princeton, NJ: Princetion University Press.

Durkheim, Emile. [1897] 1979. *Suicide: A Study in Sociology*. Translated by J. A. Spaulding and G. Simpson. New York: The Free Press.

Elifson, Kirk W., David M. Petersen, and C. Kirk Hadaway. 1983. "Religiosity and Delinquency: A Contextual Analysis." *Criminology* 21:505-527.

Ellision, Christopher G. 1991. "An Eye for an Eye? A Note on the Sourthern Subculture of Violence Thesis." *Social Forces* 69:1223-1239.

Ellision, Christopher G., Jeffrey A. Burr, and Patricia L. McCall. 1997. "Religious Homogeneity and Metropolitan Suicide Rates." *Social Forces* 76:273-299.

—. 2003. "The Enduring Puzzle of Southern Homicide: Is Regional Religious Culture the Missing Piece?" *Homicide Studies* 7:326 - 352.

Evans, T. David, Francis T. Cullen, Gregory Dunaway, and Jr. Burton, Velmer S. . 1995. "Religion and Crime Reexamined: The Impact of Religion, Secular Controls, and Social Ecology on Adult Criminality." *Criminology* 33:195-224.

Faupel, Charles E., Gregory S. Kowalski, and Paul D. Starr. 1987. "Sociology's One Law: Religion and Suicide in the Urban Context." *Journal for the Scientific Study of Religion* 26:523-534.

Federal Bureau of Investigation. 2011. "Murder." vol. 2011.

Felson, Marcus and Rachel Boba. 2010. *Crime and Everyday Life*. Thousand Oaks, CA: Sage Publications.

Felson, Richard B. and Henry J. Steadman. 1983. "Situational Factors in Disputes Leading to Criminal Violence." *Criminology* 21:59-74.

Fernquist, Robert M. 2002. "Lethal Violence Rates and Suicide-Homicide Ratios in 21 Developed Countries, 1955-1994: How Different are LVR and SHR from Suicide and Homicide Rates?" *Archives of Suicide Research* 6:237-247.

Finke, Roger and Christopher P. Scheitle. 2005. "Accounting for the Uncounted: Computing Correctives for the 2000 RCMS Data." *Review of Religious Research* 47:5-22.

Fox, James Alan. 2006. "Demographics and U.S. Homicide." Pp. 288-317 in *The Crime Drop In America: Revised Edition*, edited by A. Blumstein and J. Wallman. New York: Cambridge University Press.

Fox, James Alan and Alex R. Piquero. 2003. "Deadly Demographics: Population Characteristics and Forecasting Homicide Trends." *Crime & Delinquency* 49:339-359.

Frendreis, John and Raymond Tatalovich. 2010. ""A Hundred Miles of Dry": Religion and the Persistence of Prohibition in the U.S. States." *State Politics and Policy Quarterly* 10:302-319.

—. 2011. "Validating Protestant Denominational Classifications Using the Chaves Inerrancy Scale." *Politics and Religion* 4:355-365.

Gearing, Robin E. and Dana Lizardi. 2009. "Religion and Suicide." *Journal of Religion and Health* 48:332-341.

Gold, Martin. 1958. "Suicide, Homicide, and the Socialization of Aggression." *American Journal of Sociology* 63:651-661.

Grasmick, Harold G., Elizabeth Davenport, Mitchell B. Chamlin, and Robert J. Bursik, Jr. 1992. "Protestant Fundamentalism and the Retributive Doctrine of Punishment." *Criminology* 30:21-45.

Guerry, André-Michel. [1833] 2002. *Essay on the Moral Statistics of France*, vol. 26. Translated by H. P. Whitt and V. W. Reinking. Lewiston, NY: Edwin Mellen Press.

Hammond, W. Rodney, Daniel J. Whitaker, John R. Lutzker, James Mercy, and Pamela M. Chin. 2006. "Setting a Violence Prevention Agenda at the Centers for Disease Control and Prevention." *Aggression and Violent Behavior* 11:112-119.

He, Ni, Liqun Cao, William Wells, and Edward Maguire. 2003. "Forces of Production and Direction: A Test of an Expanded Model of Suicide and Homicide." *Homicide Studies* 7:36-57.

Henry, Andrew F. and Jr. Short, James F. 1954. *Suicide and Homicide: some economic, sociological and psychological aspects of aggression*. London: Collier-Macmillan.

Hertz, Marci Feldman, Deborah Prothrow-Stith, and Clementina Chery. 2009. "Homicide Survivors: Research and Practice Implications." *American Journal of Preventive Medicine* 29:288-295.

Higgins, Paul C. and Gary L. Albrecht. 1977. "Hellfire and Delinquency Revisited." *Social Forces* 55:952-958.

Hirsch, Jameson K. 2006. "A Review of the Literature of Rural Suicide: Risk and Protective Factors, Incidence, and Prevention." *Crisis* 27:189-199.

Hirschi, Travis and Rodney Stark. 1969. "Hellfire and Delinquency." *Social Problems* 17:202-213.

Hoffmann, John P. and Stephen J. Bahr. 2006. "Crime/Deviance." Pp. 241-263 in *Handbook of religion and social institutions*, edited by H. R. Ebaugh. New York: Springer.

Hummer, Robert A., Christopher G. Ellision, Richard G. Rogers, Benjamin E. Moulton, and Ron R. Romero. 2004. "Religious Involvement and Adult Mortality in the United States: Review and Perspective." *Southern Medical Journal* 97:1223-1230.

Jensen, Gary F. 2006. "Religious Cosmologies and Homicide Rates Among Nations: A Closer Look." *Journal of Religion and Society* 8:1-14.

Johnson, Byron R., Spencer De Li, David B. Larson, and Michael McCullough. 2000. "A Systematic Review of the Religiosity and Delinquency Literature: A Research Note." *Journal of Contemporary Criminal Justice* 16:32-52.

Johnson, Byron R. and Sung Joon Jang. 2010. "Crime and Religion: Assessing the Role of the Faith Factor." Pp. 117-149 in *American Society of Criminology*, edited by R. Rosenfeld, K. Quinet, and C. Garcia. San Francisco, CA: Wadsworth.

Jones, Dale E., Sherri Doty, James E. Horsch, Richard Houseal, Mac Lynn, John P. Marcum, Kenneth M. Sanchagrin, and Richard H. Taylor. 2002. "Religious Congregations and Membership in the United States 2000: An Enumeration by Religion, State and County Based on Data Reported by 149 Religious Bodies." Nashville, TN: Glenmary Research Center.

Knudten, Richard D. and Mary S. Knudten. 1971. "Juvenile Delinquency, Crime, and Religion." *Review of Religious Research* 12:130-152.

Kowalski, Gregory S. and Don Duffield. 1990. "The Impact of the Rural Population Component on Homicide Rates in the United States: A County-Level Analysis." *Rural Sociology* 55:76-90.

Kowalski, Gregory S., Charles E. Faupel, and Paul D. Starr. 1987. "Urbanism and Suicide: A Study of American Counties." *Social Forces* 66:85-101.

Kposowa, Augustine J. and Kevin D. Breault. 1993. "Reassessing the Structural Covariates of U.S. Homicide Rates: A County Level Study." *Sociological Focus* 26:27 - 46.

Kposowa, Augustine J., Kevin D. Breault, and Beatrice M. Harrison. 1995. "Reassessing the Structural Covariates of Violent and Property Crimes in the USA: A County Level Analysis." *British Jouranl of Sociology* 46:79-105.

Land, Kenneth C., Patricia L. McCall, and Lawrence E. Cohen. 1990. "Structural Covariates of Homicide Rates: Are there Any Invariances across Time and Social Space?" *American Journal of Sociology* 95:922 - 963.

Lanier, Christina. 2010. "Structure, Culture, and Lethality: An integrated Model Approach to American Indian Suicide and Homicide." *Homicide Studies* 14:72-89.

Lee, Matthew R. 2006. "The Religious Institutional Base and Violent Crime in Rural Areas." *Journal for the Scientific Study of Religion* 45:309 - 324.

Lee, Matthew R., William B. Bankston, Timothy C. Hayes, and Shaun A. Thomas. 2007. "Revisiting the Southern Culture of Violence." *Sociological Quarterly* 48:253-275.

Lee, Matthew R. and John Bartkowski, P. 2004a. "Civic Participation, Regional Subcultures, and Violence: The Differential Effects of Secular and Religious Participation on Adult and Juvenile Homicide." *Homicide Studies* 8:5-39.

—. 2004b. "Love Thy Neighbor? Moral Communities, Civic Engagement, and Juvenile Homicide in Rural Areas." *Social Forces* 82:1001-1035.

Lester, David and Antoon A. Leenaars. 1998. "Is There a Regional Subculture of Firearm Violence in Canada?" *Medical Science and Law* 38:317-320.

Lester, David and Bijou Yang. 1998. *Suicide and Homicide in the 20th Century: Changes Over Time*. Commack, NY: Nova Science Publishers, Inc. .

Luckenbill, David F. 1977. "Criminal Homicide as a Situated Transaction." *Social Problems* 25:176-186.

McCall, Patricia L., Kenneth C. Land, and Karen F. Parker. 2010. "An Empirical Assessment of What We Know About Structual Covariates of Homicide Rates: A Return to a Classic 20 Years Later." *Homicide Studies* 14:219-243.

McCollister, Kathryn E., Michael T. French, and Hai Fang. 2010. "The Cost of Crime to Society: New Crime-Specific Estimates for Policy and Program Evaluation." *Drug and Alcohol Dependence* 108:98-109.

McKeown, Robert E., Steven P. Cuffe, and Richard M. Schulz. 2006. "U.S. Suicide Rates by Age Group, 1970-2002: An Examination of Recent Trends." *American Journal of Public Health* 96:1745-1751.

Mencken, F. Carson, Christopher Bader, and Elizabeth Embry. 2009. "In God We Trust: Images of God and Trust in the United States Among The Highly Religious." *Sociological Perspectives* 52:23-38.

Mercy, James A., Etienne G. Krug, Linda L. Dahlberg, and Anthony B. Zwi. 2003. "Violence and Health: The United States in a Global Perspective." *American Journal of Public Health* 92:256-261.

Messner, Steven F., Eric P. Baumer, and Richard Rosenfeld. 2004. "Dimensions of Social Capital and Rates of Criminal Homicide." *American Sociological Review* 69:882-903.

Miethe, Terance D. and Robert F. Meier. 1994. *Crime and its social context: Toward an integrated theory of offenders, victims, and situations*. Albany, NY: SUNY Press.

Miller, Matthew, Deborah Azrael, and David Hemenway. 2002. "Rates of Household Firearm Ownership and Homicide Across U.S. Regions and States, 1988-1997." *American Journal of Public Health* 92:1988-1993.

Minino, Arialdi M., Sherry L. Murphy, Jiaquan Xu, and Kenneth D. Kochanek. 2011. "Deaths: Final Data for 2008." vol. 59, edited by Division of Vital Statistics. Hayttsville, MD: National Center for Health Statistics.

Morse, Steven. 2004. *Indices and Indicators in Development: An Unhealthy Obsession with Numbers.* Stirling, VA: Earthscan.

Morselli, Enrico. [1881] 1903. *Suicide: An Essay on Comparative Moral Statistics*, vol. 36. New York: D. Appleton and Company.

Nielsen, Amie L. and Ramiro Martinez, Jr. . 2009. "The role of immigration for violent deaths." *Homicide Studies* 13:274-287.

Norstrom, Thor. 2011. "Alcohol and Homicide in the United States: Is the Link Dependent on Wetness?" *Drug and Alcohol Review* 30:458-465.

O'Brien, Robert M. and Jean Stockard. 2006. "A Common Explanation for the Changing Age Distributions of Suicide and Homicide in the United States, 1930 to 2000." *Social Forces* 84:1539-1557.

Osgood, D. Wayne. 2000. "Poisson-Based Regression Analysis of Aggregate Crime Rates." *Journal of Quantitative Criminology* 16:21-43.

Osgood, D. Wayne and Jeff M. Chambers. 2000. "Social Disorganization Outside the Metropolis: An Analysis of Rural Youth Violence." *Criminology* 38:81-116.

Papadopoulos, Fotios C., Alkistis Skalkidou, Theodoros N. Sergentanis, Spyros Kyllekidis, Lisa Ekselius, and Eleni Th. Petridou. 2009. "Preventing Suicide and Homicide in the United States: The Potential Benefit in Human Lives." *Psychiatry Research* 169:154-158.

Parker, Karen F., Patricia L. McCall, and Kenneth C. Land. 1999. "Determining Social-Structural Pedictors of Homicide: Units of Analysis and Related Methodological Concerns." Pp. 107 - 124 in *Homicide: A Sourcebook of Social Research*, edited by M. D. Smith and M. A. Zahn. Thousand Oaks: Sage.

Pearce, Lisa D. and Dana L. Haynie. 2004. "Intergenerational Religious Dynamics and Adolescent Delinquency." *Social Forces* 82:1553 - 1572.

Pescosolido, Bernice A. 1990. "The Social Context of Religious Integration and Suicide: Pursuing the Network Explanation." *The Sociological Quarterly* 31:337-357.

—. 1994. "Bringing Durkheim into the Twenty-First Century: A Network Approach to Unresolved Issues in the Sociology of Suicide." Pp. 264-295 in *Emile Durkheim Le Suicide 100 Years Later*, edited by D. Lester. Philadelphia: Charles Press.

Pescosolido, Bernice A. and Sharon Georgianna. 1989. "Durkheim, Suicide, and Religion: Toward a Network Theory of Suicide." *American Sociological Review* 54:33-48.

Pescosolido, Bernice A. and Robert Mendelsohn. 1986. "Social Causation or Social Construction of Suicide? An Infestigation Into the Social Organization of Offical Rates." *American Sociological Review* 51:80-101.

Pridemore, William Alex. 2002. "What We Know About Social Structure and Homicide: A Review of the Theoretical and Emprical Literature." *Violence and Victims* 17:127-156.

—. 2005. "A Cautionary Note on Using County-Level Crime and Homicide Data." *Homicide Studies* 9:256-268.

Putnam, Robert D. and David E. Campbell. 2010. *American Grace: How Religion Divides and Unites Us*. New York: Simon & Schuster.

Regnerus, Mark D. 2003. "Moral Communities and Adolescent Delinquency: Religious Contexts and Community Social Control." *The Sociological Quarterly* 44:523-554.

Rezaeian, Mohsen. 2008. "Suicide/Homicide Ratios in Countries of the Eastern Mediterranean Region." *Eastern Mediterranean Health Journal* 14:1459-1465.

—. 2011. "An Analysis of WHO Data on Lethal Violence: Relevance of the New Western Millennium." *Asia-Pacific Journal of Public Health* 23:163-170.

Richardson, Erin G. and David Hemenway. 2011. "Homicide, Suicide, and Unintentional Firearm Fatality: Comparing the United States With Other High-Income Countries, 2003." *The Journal of Trauma Injury, Infection, and Critical Care* 70:238-243.

Rivera, Craig, Rebekah Chu, and Colin Loftin. 2002. "Do Strong Communities Increase Homicide? An Evaluation of the Nisbett-Cohen Thesis." *International Journal of Sociology and Social Policy* 22:109-121.

Robins, Alee and Amy Fiske. 2009. "Explaining the Relation between Religiousness and Reduced Suicidal Behavior: Social Support Rather Than Specific Beliefs." *Suicide and Life-Threatening Behavior* 39:386-395.

Robinson, W. S. 1950. "Ecological Correlations and the Behavior of Individuals." *American Sociological Review* 15:351-357.

Rockett, Ian R. H. 1998. "Injury and Violence: A Public Health Perspective." *Population Bulletin* 53:3-39.

Rosenberg, M. L., L. E. Davidson, J. C. Smith, A. L. Berman, H. Buzbee, G. Gantner, G. A. Gay, B. More-Lewis, D. H. Mills, and D. Murray. 1988. "Operational Criteria for the Determination of Suicide." *Journal of Forensic Sciences* 33:1445-1456.

Rosenberg, Mark L., Patrick W. O'Carroll, and Kenneth E. Powell. 1992. "Let's Be Clear: Violence Is a Public Health Problem." *Journal of the American Medical Association* 267:3071-3072.

Rosenfeld, Richard, Steven F. Messner, and Eric P. Baumer. 2001. "Social Capital and Homicide." *Social Forces* 80:283-309.

Sampson, Robert J. and W. Byron Groves. 1989. "Community Structure and Crime: Testing Social-Disorganization Theory." *American Journal of Sociology* 94:774-802.

Sampson, Robert J., Jeffrey D. Morenoff, and Felton Earls. 1999. "Beyond Social Capital: Spatial Dynamics of Collective Efficacy for Childern." *American Sociological Review* 64:633-660.

Sampson, Robert J., Steven W. Raudenbush, and Felton Earls. 1997. "Neighborhoods and Violent Crime: A Multilevel Study of Collective Efficacy." *Science* 277.

Shihadeh, Edward S. and Lisa Winters. 2010. "Church, Place, and Crime: Latinos and Homicide in New Destinations." *Sociological Inquiry* 80:628-649.

Shrira, Ilan and Nicholas Christenfeld. 2010. "Disentangling the Person and the Place as Explanations for Regional Differences in Suicide." *Suicide and Life-Threatening Behavior* 40:287-297.

Singh, Gopal K. 2002. "Increasing Rural--Urban Gradients in U.S. Suicide Mortality, 1970--1997." *American Journal of Public Health* 92:1161-1167.

Singh, Raghu N. and N. Prabha Unnithan. 1999. "Wife Burning: Cultural Cues for Lethal Violence Against Women Among Asian Indians in the United States." *Violence Against Women* 5:641-653.

Sloane, Douglas M. and Raymond H. Potvin. 1986. "Religion and Delinquency: Cutting Through the Maze." *Social Forces* 65:87-105.

South, Scott J. 1987. "Metropolitan Migration and Social Problems." *Social Science Quarterly* 68:3-18.

Stack, Steven. 1983. "The Effect of the Decline in Institutionalized Religion on Suicide, 1954-1978." *Journal for the Scientific Study of Religion* 22:239-252.

—. 2000a. "Suicide: A 15-Year Review of the Sociological Literature Part I: Cultural and Economic Factors." *Suicide and Life-Threatening Behavior* 30:145-162.

—. 2000b. "Suicide: A 15-Year Review of the Sociological Literature Part II: Modernization and Social Integration Perspectives." *Suicide and Life-Threatening Behavior* 30:163-176.

Stark, Rodney. 1996. "Religion as Context: Hellfire and Delinquency One More Time." *Sociology of Religion* 57:163-173.

Stark, Rodney and William Sims Bainbridge. 1996. *Religion, Deviance, and Social Control*. New York: Routledge.

Stark, Rodney, Daniel P. Doyle, and Jesse Lynn Rushing. 1983. "Beyond Durkheim: Religion and Suicide." *Journal for the Scientific Study of Religion* 22:120-131.

Stark, Rodney, Lori Kent, and Daniel P. Doyle. 1982. "Religion and Delinquency: the Ecology of a "Lost" Relationship." *Journal of Research in Crime and Delinquency* 19:4-24.

Stockard, Jean. 2003. "Social Science, Social Policy, and Lethal Violence: Looking for Upstream Solutions: 2003 Presidential Address to the Pacific Sociological Association." *Sociological Perspectives* 46:291-308.

Tcherni, Maria. 2011. "Structural Determinats of Homicide: The Big Three." *Journal of Quantitative Criminology* 27:475-496.

Timmermans, Stefan. 2005. "Suicide Determination and the Professional Authority of Medical Examiners." *American Sociological Review* 70:311-333.

Tittle, Charles R. and Michael R. Welch. 1983. "Religiosity and Deviance: Toward a Contingency of Constraining Effects." *Social Forces* 61:653-682.

Ulmer, Jeffery T., Christopher Bader, and Martha Gault. 2008. "Do Moral Communities Play A Role In Criminal Sentencing? Evidence from Pennsylvania." *The Sociological Quarterly* 49:737-768.

Unnithan, N. Prabha, Lin Huff-Corzine, Jay Corzine, and Hugh P. Whitt. 1994. *The Currents of Lethal Violence: An Integrated Model of Suicide and Homicide*. Albany: State University of New York.

Vollum, Scott and Victoria Brewer Titterington. 2001. "Gender, Attributional Styles, and Direction of Lethal Violence: A Partial Test of an Integrated Model of Suicide and Homicide." *Homicide Studies* 5:227-252.

Walker, Jacob T. 2009. "County Level Suicide Rates and Social Integration: Urbanicity and Its Role in the Relationship." *Sociological Spectrum* 29:101-135.

Weisheit, Ralph A. and L. Edwards Wells. 2005. "Deadly Violence in the Heartland: Comparing Homicide Patterns in Nonmetropolitan and Metropolitan Counties." *Homicide Studies* 9:55 - 80.

Whitt, Hugh P. 2006. "Where Did the Bodies Go? The Social Construciton of Suicide Data, New York City, 1976--1992." *Sociological Inquiry* 76:166-187.

Wiersema, Brian, Colin Loftin, and David McDowall. 2000. "A Comparison of Supplementary Homicide Reports and National Vital Statistics System Homicide Estimates for U.S. Counties." *Homicide Studies* 4:317-340.

Wolfgang, Marvin E. 1958. *Patterns in Criminal Homicide*. Oxford: Universit of Pennsylvania Press.

Wray, Matt, Cynthia Colen, and Bernice Pescosolido. 2011. "The Sociology of Suicide." *Annual Review of Sociology* 37:505-528.

Wu, Bohsiu. 2003. "Testing the Stream Analogy for Lethal Violence: A Macro Study of Suicide and Homicide." *Western Criminology Review* 4:215-225.

—. 2004. "Testing Three Competing Hypotheses for Explaining Lethal Violence." *Violence and Victims* 19:399-411.

Zimring, Franklin E. and Gordon Hawkins. 1997. *Crime is Not the Problem: Lethal Violence in America*. New York: Oxford University Press.

Index

M

N

P

R

S

U